Network South

David Brown and

Capital Transport

ISBN 185414 129 5

Published by Capital Transport Publishing
38 Long Elmes, Harrow Weald, Middlesex

Printed by Hastings Printing Company, Hastings, Sussex

Information in this book is correct to November 1990 and it is hoped to publish the next edition towards the end of 1992. While it is not an official publication of Network SouthEast, we should like to thank NSE's Public Affairs Office for their help during its compilation. Thanks are also due to Piers Connor, Hugh Dady, Alex Dasi-Sutton, Brian Morrison, Dick Riley and Chris Wilson.

The front cover photograph of two 313s at South Acton and the lower photograph on page one of a 455 unit at Ashtead are by David Brown; the back cover photograph of a 315 approaching Hackney Downs station is by Chris Wilson; the upper photograph on page one and the photographs on pages four and five were supplied by Network SouthEast.

Contents

Network SouthEast
An Introduction

Network SouthEast is one of the five Business Sectors of British Rail, and is concerned with operating passenger services in London and the South East of England, over one of the most complex urban rail systems in the World. The hub of the network is London, but it stretches as far as King's Lynn at its North Eastern extent and Weymouth and Exeter at its South Western extremities. It is prime user of (and therefore financially responsible for) just over 2000 route miles of line, of which 75% are electrified on one of two systems, and also operates some services over a further 500 miles of InterCity sponsored track. It operates its services with about 7000 vehicles, and employs a staff of approximately 41,000. There are 942 stations on the Network, ranging in size from the huge 21-platform Clapham Junction to tiny wayside halts such as Morden Road.

The majority of services Network SouthEast operates are suburban or outer-suburban in character and London commuting forms the major traffic flows; indeed in 1989 nearly half a million passengers commuted into the Capital between 07 00 and 10 00 on each weekday, and a train arrived in London during the morning peak on average every 11 seconds! However, as will be seen in the chapters that follow, Network SouthEast is a surprisingly varied operation, in terms of rolling stock, routes and stations.

An Historical Perspective

The first railway in London was the London and Greenwich, which opened between Deptford and Spa Road in February 1836, and throughout by 1840. It was followed by a large number of other companies, bringing in lines from all directions and eventually connecting London to virtually all parts of the British mainland. Local traffic in the London area was served either by intermediate stations on the main lines, or by separate routes off the main lines. Some of the main-line companies, particularly those concerned with working long-distance services such as the Great Northern, treated this local traffic as little more than a necessary nuisance. Other railway companies, particularly those with only short main line routes, such as the Great Eastern (GER) and London, Brighton and South Coast (LBSC) actively courted local and suburban traffic, building new lines and stations to stimulate suburban growth and thus generate extra revenue. Whole areas of London inner suburbia, such as Walthamstow, owe their existence to the Railway.

As a result of Government policy during the 'Railway Mania' of the 1840s, virtually all the main-line railway companies were forced to terminate on the edge of the City, and passengers wishing to travel between the termini were forced to do so on foot or by expensive horse-bus or taxi. While the railway was the sole means of transport over any distance, use was made of many odd spurs and connections to provide direct local services between two places around the metropolis, albeit often circuitous in the extreme! For example, at one time GWR trains from the West worked into Victoria, while the London and South Western took its customers from Kensington to Richmond via a very roundabout route through Shepherd's Bush and Hammersmith! Customers used these inconvenient services purely because there was little choice, but quickly abandoned them when more convenient means of conveyance were introduced.

In 1863 the first of London's underground railways, the Metropolitan, was opened. In the built-up area it generally ran in covered trenches under the streets and its network of lines steadily expanded, later being joined by others including the deep-level 'tube' lines, the first of which opened in 1890. Not surprisingly, these new underground railways provided direct connections between the main-line termini, and together with the introduction of electric trams and motor buses caused a severe decline in traffic on the inner suburban lines of the main line companies in the first years of the Twentieth Century. As a result, routes were rationalised and stations closed, a process which came to a head during World War I. Steps were also taken to economise in operation and make remaining services more popular, notably by electrification. Conversely, commuting from towns outside the built-up area into London was increasing at this time.

Ironically, of the main-line companies, only the impoverished London, Chatham and Dover Railway managed to build a line through from north to south, opening its Metropolitan extension from Ludgate Hill to Farringdon Street in 1874. At the latter station it made a junction with the 'Widened Lines' of the Metropolitan Railway, which had connections onto the lines of the Great Northern and Midland Railways. The passenger service along this useful connection ceased in 1916; it reopened in 1988 and now provides the route for Thameslink services.

The many railway companies were all amalgamated into four larger companies in the Grouping of 1923. The new concerns were the Southern Railway (SR), the Great Western Railway (GWR), the London, Midland and Scottish Railway (LMS) and the London and North Eastern Railway (LNER). The period between the two World Wars saw the expansion of suburban London in a big way, economic conditions being favourable to the speculative construction of housing estates and whole new communities sprang up, added to by huge new housing estates put up by the London County Council, such as St Helier. The number of owner-occupiers commuting into London increased dramatically. The Southern Railway, with its many short-distance routes and ever-heavier suburban traffic, took the initiative regarding modernisation to cater for this increase in traffic. Under its capable General Manager Herbert Walker, virtually the entire SR suburban network and a number of medium-distance routes to the coast were electrified. This was one factor stimulating the house-building boom in the suburbs, and the heavy increase in commuting brought increased profits for the shareholders. Whole new suburbs, such as Stoneleigh and Albany Park, grew up around new stations, often provided as a joint venture with the builders. Two entirely new lines, from Wimbledon to Sutton and from Motspur Park to Chessington, were constructed in this period to service existing and stimulate new suburban development.

The other railway companies were somewhat more reticent about catering for these trends, partly due to lack of money, and partly due to concentrating resources on prime long-distance routes which the SR did not really have. On the second-busiest suburban network around London, the Great Eastern section of the LNER, an intensive steam-hauled operation continued, no money being available for electrification. The other main-line companies, the LMS and GWR, had much smaller suburban operations, and likewise remained wedded to steam power. An exception was the LMS Watford 'New' line, previously electrified by the LNWR, and on this route a few new stations were opened. Much of the expansion in the northern suburbs was left to the Underground lines, often in competition with the main line companies, but sometimes in partnership with them, whereby tube lines were extended over former Main Line branches. The GWR and LNER in particular managed to off-load some of their suburban operations to London Transport in this way, although work on these extensions (High Barnet and Mill Hill East, Hainault, Epping and Ongar, West Ruislip) was not completed until well after World War II.

The four main-line railway companies, with their disparate suburban services around the Capital, were nationalised by the Labour Government then in power as from 1st January 1948. Of the six new 'Regions' which replaced the old Companies as Management entities, those which operated suburban services into and around London and the Home Counties included the Southern, Eastern, London Midland and Western. As will be related in later chapters, SR standards tended to prevail, both in terms of livery (sombre dark green for the majority of suburban stock) and in carriage design, especially the vast amounts of new rolling stock produced under the 1955 Modernisation Plan. But otherwise the Regions largely went their own way – there was little interface between the various suburban systems north and south of the Thames. The British Rail corporate image of 1965 failed to change much in terms of services, although the previous regional house colours gradually disap-peared to be replaced by an all-enveloping blue (relieved by a light grey window band on main line stock, later extended to all trains) colour scheme for rolling stock and black-on-white station nameboards.

With the Conservative Government under Prime Minister Margaret Thatcher in office from 1979, a much more businesslike approach to the running of the railways was adopted, primarily to reduce the call on the public purse (£281 million came from the taxpayer to support rail services in the South East in the year before NSE came into being). As part of this approach, British Rail was divided into five business sectors as from 4th January 1982: these were InterCity, London and South East, Provincial (renamed Regional Railways in 1990), Railfreight and Parcels. These new arrangements were the brainchild of Sir Robert Reid, Chairman of the BRB and one of the few to come from inside the railway hierarchy since Nationalisation.

Creation of the London and South East sector meant that for the first time a single organisation planned the surface railways' passenger business in the London region, allowing a properly integrated approach to the marketing and planning of passenger services for the capital. To start with, the Directorship of the new Sector was combined with General Managership of Southern Region, which formed by far its largest part, and the original incumbent of the post was therefore David Kirby. At first, the new organisation was fairly low-key as far as the travelling public were concerned, most of the new initiatives and developments, such as the 1986 Hastings via Tonbridge electrification ("Ride The 1066 Electrics"), being still promoted by the relevant BR Region. However, some moves were planned towards an L&SE image, particularly with new rolling stock liveries and upholstery moquette patterns. The Main Line two-tone brown livery with orange dividing stripe, quickly dubbed 'jaffa cake', was much in evidence on Kent Coast class 411 '4 Cep' stock until mid-1990, and was also applied to certain Brighton Line class 421 '4 Cig' and Clacton class 309 EMUs for a short time. The proposed outer- and inner-suburban colour schemes, two-tone blue and two-tone green respectively, both with dividing orange stripe, did not get beyond the drawing board – perhaps thankfully! The new moquette patterns, again characterised by an orange stripe, were all produced however, being used well into the NSE era. The brown- and blue-based designs were for first and second (now standard) class seating respectively in main line stock. The green-based pattern is somewhat rarer, being used only in refurbished SR class 415 and 416 'EPB' and Anglia Region class 305/1 'Chingford' suburban units.

In mid-1985, the L&SE Sector Directorship was split from the SR General Managership, the latter job going to Gordon Pettitt (since promoted to the post of Sector Director, Provincial, and replaced on the SR by John Ellis). In November of that year David Kirby was promoted to the British Railways Board, his place being taken by Chris Green.

Probably the most dynamic British railway manager of recent times, Chris Green was educated at St Pauls and Oxford, and joined BR as a Management Trainee in Birmingham in 1965. Working his way through various Management posts around the country, he eventually became Regional Operations Manager on Scottish Region in 1980, Deputy General Manager in 1983 and General Manager of the Region, by now dubbed ScotRail, a year later. By developing a much greater public awareness, Mr Green brought new prosperity to rail services in Scotland, and the result was new and refurbished stations, lines reopened and improved timetables. Part of his technique was to utilise a very eye-catching, even brash, visual image to give the railways in Scotland their own identity. In view of his success on Scotrail, he was an obvious candidate for the task of revitalising the somewhat downtrodden London and South East rail network, the largest of the BR's sectors. Away from the railway, Chris Green is married with a daughter, and lists his interests as hill walking, travel, architecture, theatre, music and reading.

For the launch of Network SouthEast on 10th June 1986, a number of stations had been repainted, re-signed and otherwise refurbished to give customers some idea of what to expect from the new administration. These were spread out over the Network area to give as many passengers as possible a glimpse of things to come on that first day. They included Waterloo, Richmond, Purley, Blackheath and Chatham on Southern Region, Radlett, Harrow and Wealdstone, Hemel Hempstead, Denham and the suburban platforms at Euston on London Midland Region, Barking, Finsbury Park and Shenfield on Eastern Region (as was) and Hayes & Harlington on Western Region. A selection of rolling stock had been painted (in some secrecy!) in the new red, white and blue colour scheme. These included examples of locomotives of classes 47/4 and 50, a class 115 DMU, electric units of classes 310, 313, 315, 317, 423 and 455, and various hauled coaches. Again, after the morning Press launch at Waterloo all were run in service to give as many passengers as possible a sight of the new image. Internally the trains were equipped with various new upholstery patterns, NSE and London Connections maps, and advertising. The adverts (all for American Express) did not last; the other features have proved more durable.

Above **A distinctive Network image has been established by extensive renewal of signing and other station furnishings in addition to the eye-catching livery adopted for rolling stock.** Capital Transport

Left **Chris Green, Director, Network SouthEast.**

Aims and Objectives

Financial: First and foremost, the objective of Network SouthEast has been to make the railways around London more financially efficient, in line with Government objectives to reduce the call on public finances. Since 1979, BR has been subject to meeting financial performance targets agreed between the BR Board and the Department of Transport. Since its formation, NSE has always managed to meet or better these targets, and in its first three years (1986-89) Government support in the form of the Public Services Obligation Grant (PSO, to underwrite loss-making but socially necessary public transport services) was halved. In December 1989, the new Minister of Transport announced that, as part of the next five-year plan for BR, Network SouthEast was expected to break even by 1992-93. If this is achieved, NSE will be the first urban railway in the World to operate without Government subsidy for many years. The Government may still however give grants for specific investments to improve the system, but such grants are subject to stringent financial scrutiny.

Service: While reducing the need for subsidy, it has been NSE policy from the start to improve the quality of the service it offers, both to ease the lot of the long-suffering commuter and to encourage more business both peak and off-peak. The rise in such traffic increases revenue to pay for investment in new rolling stock, rebuilt stations etc, while reducing the call on the public purse, and this was the cornerstone of Network Policy at the start. Incentives such as the Network Card, One Day Travelcard, 'Network Days' and the various special promotions and events are all designed to tempt customers onto the railway and fill otherwise empty seats on trains.

Included in the 'Manifesto' of the 1986 launch of Network SouthEast were various stated objectives regarding Quality of Service, invariably better than what had gone before, and designed to go some way towards meeting the most common complaints about rail travel from customers. For example:-

Punctuality Objective: 90% of trains arriving on time or within 5 minutes.
Service Provision Objective: At least 99% of advertised services to be operated.
Train Enquiry Bureaux Objective: At least 95% of calls to be answered within 30 seconds.
Ticket Offices Objective: Maximum queuing time of three minutes off-peak and five minutes peak.
Carriage Cleaning Objective: 100% Daily interior and exterior clean. 100% heavy interior clean every 28 days.

While it cannot truthfully be stated that all these objectives have been met so far, it may be said that NSE has gone a long way to meeting them, in spite of difficult circumstances. Standards vary between particular routes; an advantage of the recently introduced 'Route Management' is that problems or substandard service on a particular line may quickly be identified and appropriate action taken.

There are particular problems in meeting some of these objectives on some parts of NSE. Staff recruitment is difficult due to unsocial hours and the cost of housing, and this contributes to cancellation of trains. The age of some rolling stock causes unreliability, and this also leads to a reduction in service. This latter problem is being overcome by investment in new trains at the highest level since the 1950s. Some problems are caused as a result of factors completely out of NSE's control. For example, the drought of 1989 meant that carriage washing machines in Kent could not be used; this resulted in trains which were nothing short of filthy.

Investment: Investment in new trains, electrification and stations doubled in the first three years of NSE's existence, and is presently running at £1 million per day. Details are described later.

Management Structure

It must be remembered that Network SouthEast is a commercially-led organisation, and the management structure reflects this. Under the Sector Director is a Deputy Director and separate managers responsible for strategy (major investment decisions and product development) in the following areas:-

a) Public Relations
b) Strategic Planning
c) Marketing
d) Finance
e) Resources and Investment
f) Quality
g) Terminals

Also responsible to the Director are the six Network Managers each in charge of a particular area, known as a subsector. Since 1989, each subsector has been further divided into routes, each of which has been given a local identify by using a 'brand name' and distinctive badge; each route has a route manager responsible to the particular area Network Manager. Network and route managers are responsible for setting and monitoring product (eg train service) quality standards, investment scheme development and local marketing. Further details of route branding are given in the following section, but the areas and the routes which come into them are as follows:-

Subsector	Routes
Anglia	Great Eastern
	London, Tilbury and Southend
	West Anglia
	Great Northern Lines
North	Northampton Line
	Thameslink
	North London Lines
	Three Counties
South Central	South London Lines
	Sussex Coast
	Oxted Line
South East	Kent Link
	Kent Coast
	Marsh Link
South West	South Western Lines
	Solent and Wessex
	West of England
	Island Line
	Waterloo and City
Thames and Chiltern	Thames
	Chiltern

The actual physical operation of the railway is under the responsibility of Regional Management, the Regions being contracted by NSE to provide a particular level of service on a particular route. Regional management is responsible for personnel recruitment, rolling stock maintenance etc, all of which can be called the 'operations' or 'production' aspect of running the railway. In some cases, the 'ownership' of a particular service is rather more concerned with financial performance than geographical logic. For example, the rural service to King's Lynn, well out of England's 'South East', is owned by NSE and the route is presently being electrified. The profitable Gatwick Express to and from Victoria on the other hand is owned by InterCity, despite operating in the very heartland of the Network.

Route Branding

A development in the Management Structure of the NSE during 1989 was the introduction of Line Management, each line or group of lines being the responsibility of a commercial manager answerable to the sub-sector manager. A route identity hopefully increases staff morale, and allows problems to be more easily identified and more quickly acted upon. Where services cross regional or area boundaries, the introduction of line management has made the running of the railway a far simpler and more efficient process – the North London Link between Richmond and North Woolwich, for example, has been transformed. Coincidental with the introduction of Line Management, each route has been given a name and identifying badge; apart from on the trains themselves, these also appear on timetables, advertising etc.

This Page **A selection of the Route Branding logos currently in use on Network SouthEast.**

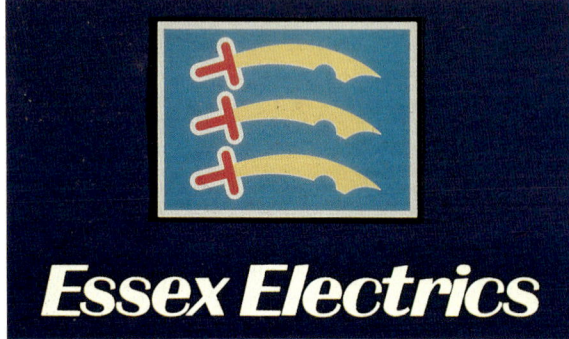

Facing Page Upper **Examples of NSE publicity. The South London Lines route and frequency guide was published in May 1990 to coincide with improved frequency on a number of South London routes.**

Facing Page Lower **Three of a series of posters designed by Edward Pond featuring places served by Network SouthEast.**

South London Lines

Route and Frequency Guide

It's fast

Frequent

Easy

14 May 1990 to 12 May 1991

Network SouthEast

Taking the train to the theatre.

THE LONDON THEATRE ACT ON IT

3 October 1988-13 May 1989

West End Theatre Travel Guide.
Details of rail travel, easy Underground
connections and late trains home.

Network SouthEast

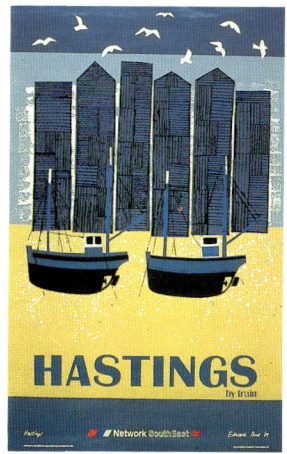

Travelling radially around the NSE area in a clockwise direction, the various routes are as follows:-

Thames
London Paddington to Reading, Oxford and Newbury: the Greenford, Windsor, Marlow and Henley branches; Oxford to Bicester.

Chiltern
London Marylebone to Aylesbury, High Wycombe and Banbury.

Thameslink
Bedford and Luton to Moorgate, Gatwick Airport, Brighton, Sevenoaks, Sutton and Guildford.

Three Counties
Kettering (Northants) to Bedford (Beds), Bedford to Bletchley (Bucks).

Northampton Line
London Euston to Milton Keynes and Northampton (some trains work through to Rugby or Birmingham New Street). Operated in conjunction with Regional Railways (Midline) beyond Northampton.

North London Lines
Euston to Watford Junction stopping service; Watford Junction to Croxley Green and St Albans Abbey; Richmond to North Woolwich.

Great Northern (inner suburban)
Moorgate and London King's Cross to Welwyn Garden City, Hertford North and Hitchin (stopping services only).

Great Northern (outer suburban)
King's Cross to Huntington, Cambridge and King's Lynn.

West Anglia
London Liverpool Street to Enfield, Chingford, Hertford East, Cambridge and Stansted Airport.

Great Eastern
Liverpool Street to Harwich, Clacton, Southend Victoria and Shenfield; Romford to Upminster; Wickford to Southminster; Witham to Braintree; Marks Tey to Sudbury.

London, Tilbury and Southend
London Fenchurch Street to Tilbury, Southend Central and Shoeburyness.

Kent Link
Suburban services from London Charing Cross, Cannon Street, St Pauls, Blackfriars and Victoria to Hayes, Dartford, Gravesend, Gillingham, Orpington and Sevenoaks; Elmers End to Addiscombe, Grove Park to Bromley North.

Kent Coast
Main line services from Charing Cross, Cannon Street, St Pauls, Blackfriars and Victoria to Maidstone, Tonbridge, Ashford, Hastings, Folkestone, Dover; Ramsgate; Paddock Wood to Maidstone and Strood; Sittingbourne to Sheerness-on-Sea.

Marsh Link
Hastings to Ashford.

South London Lines
Victoria, London Bridge and Charing Cross to Crystal Palace, Croydon, Tattenham Corner, Caterham, Wimbledon, Sutton, Epsom Downs, Epsom, Dorking and Horsham; London Bridge to Victoria, Wimbledon to West Croydon.

Sussex Coast
Main line services from Victoria and London Bridge to Brighton, Littlehampton, Bognor Regis, Portsmouth, Southampton, Eastbourne and Hastings; Brighton to Hastings and Portsmouth.

Oxted Line
Victoria and London Bridge to Oxted, East Grinstead and Uckfield.

North Downs
Reading to Redhill, Gatwick Airport and Tonbridge.

South Western Lines (Inner Suburban) London Waterloo to Dorking and Effingham Junction via Epsom, to Guildford via Cobham, to Kingston and Shepperton, the Chessington and Hampton Court branches, to Richmond Hounslow and Windsor, Clapham Junction to Kensington Olympia, Staines to Weybridge.

Waterloo and City
Waterloo to Bank.

Solent and Wessex
Express services from Waterloo to Portsmouth via Guildford and via Eastleigh, and to Southampton, Poole and Weymouth. Main line stopping and outer suburban services from Waterloo to Guildford, Alton, Portsmouth, Southampton, Wareham, Ascot and Reading.

Island Line
Ryde Pier Head to Shanklin.

West of England
Waterloo to Salisbury and Exeter.

Where all the services on a particular route run on one or two lines with their own rolling stock, such as the Great Northern and Chiltern lines, the system works well. On the Southern Region however, where there is much inter-running of stock, the idea is not so successful; for example since the May 1990 Solent area electrification, trains carrying 'Sussex Coast' can regularly be seen operating as far west as Poole, while electric trains to East Grinstead via Oxted carry South London Lines or Sussex Coast badges, but never Oxted Line, which is reserved for the few DEMUs allocated to the Uckfield trains.

Building the Network Image
The main places where the railway is brought to the public eye are the trains themselves, the stations, and publicity and advertising, including such items as timetables etc. It was decided to catch the attention of customers (or potential customers) with a purposely brash and colourful image for Network SouthEast, to counteract the somewhat staid and drab image which the railway has often had. The new image was particularly aimed at optional off-peak travellers (shoppers etc). The design work was carried out by design consultants Jordan Williams, although some of the elements, in particular lettering, date back to the 'Corporate Image' style of 1965. An early manifestation of NSE's formation was the painting of station lampposts virtually all over the system bright red, an occurrence which stimulated much comment from the media! To support the building of the image a comprehensive Network Design Manual was issued to all managers which clearly established the standards to be applied.

'Thameslink' and 'Kent Coast' NSE trains race towards Bromley South. On the left is a facelifted 423 class and on the right a dual-voltage 319 class. David Brown

Rolling Stock

The style of paintwork on rolling stock is best observed in photographs. From the solebar upwards, it consists of horizontal stripes of grey, white, red, white, blue, white and red. It seems rather complicated, but the British public were assured by the Sector Director (on a TV interview) that it costs no more to apply than the previous blue/grey scheme. Cab ends have continued to be yellow, with varying degrees of black trim around cab windows etc, while other vehicle ends are generally black. Numbering and lettering on vehicle sides is blue if it falls on a white background, or white if on top of grey, red, blue or black. Superimposed on the white strip above the windows, a thin yellow stripe denotes first class accommodation, while on classes 412 and 422 a thin red stripe denotes the buffet area.

A definite feature of the cab sides is the upsweep of the stripes, initially at a sharp angle. The width of the upswept stripes varies on different stock, to try to fit them as far as possible around windows and door recesses. On a single-car unit (eg class 122 DMMU), the upsweep at both ends on one coach looks rather silly, so on some the horizontal lines continue to the end. Since late 1987, a radius has been put on the stripe upsweeps, which is an undoubted improvement.

The locomotive livery, while similar to that of coaches, initially had a white stripe around the cab windows and a small upsweep of the stripes ending below the cab side-windows. This scheme was later altered to blue around the cab windows and no upsweep. Generally though, it is felt that NSE colours do not 'sit' particularly well on locomotives, but this will become irrelevant with the virtual elimination of locomotives from the Network fleet in the not-too-distant future.

The initial shades of blue and red were rather insipid, and quickly gave a washed out appearance. Since late 1987, the shade of blue has become darker, and the red brighter. A more recent development has been the adoption of a much lighter shade of grey on certain types of stock.

Network SouthEast livery appears to have been designed with modern (and not-so-modern) sliding-door EMU stock in mind, on which it looks particularly smart. Particularly successful in this writer's view are the class 483 Isle of Wight Replacement EMUs, refurbished from 50-year-old LT tube cars, on which NSE stripes look really good. The colours sit less well on slam-door stock, and although main line vehicles have been outshopped in it since 1986, some suburban EMU stock, such as the SR 'EPB' types, have only been receiving it since late-1988.

NSE livery on former London Underground 1938 tube stock now at work on the Isle of Wight.
David Brown

Vehicle Interiors

In contrast with the bold exterior stripes, interior décor is more muted, aiming to provide a restful experience to customers. Interior panelling is mainly in shades of beige or light grey. Areas around vestibules on sliding-door stock are sometimes in a more striking colour (presumably so that passengers unfamiliar with train travel can easily find the doors), but this sensible idea seems to have gone in and then out of favour on successive builds of stock. Thus classes 313, 315 and 319 have yellow door-areas, classes 317 and 455 have orange, but class 321 has the same light grey as elsewhere internally.

Where doors have internal customer-operated open/close push buttons, these have illuminated surrounds on the latest stock, including the class 483 on the Isle of Wight.

A particular feature of most new NSE stock is the use of large abstract murals on end partitions and in first class compartments. These are by the artist Edward Pond, and depict famous buildings and sights along the routes served by the stock concerned.

Virtually all stock built new or rebuilt since 1976 has seating with removable covers, which are cleaned annually (although obviously individual covers may be replaced as required). These help to present a much cleaner image to the insides of modern rolling stock. The Network standard is to have high-backed seating in all trains. The design has developed from that in class 317 (which had separate headrests which tended to fall off), through classes 319 and 321 (with one piece backs) to Networker (arguably a better shape). It is unfortunate that many inner-suburban EMUs built just prior to the NSE era were constructed to a lower

First class compartment interior in the proposed class 471 mock-up on display at Victoria on 8th December 1989. The seats are basically similar to those in 442s, and fabrics and surfaces are in restful shades of grey and pink. David Brown

Facing Page **Typical standard class saloon inside a class 319 vehicle, similar also to classes 321 and 456. Note the high backed seating with one-piece backs, and the Eddie Pond murals on the end walls, in this instance showing St Pauls Cathedral and Tower Bridge.** David Brown

specification with low-backed seating – these will have to remain for some time due to the uneconomic cost of replacement. First class seating is generally based on standard class seating of longer distance stock, and is of course more spaced out.

Seat upholstery fabric patterns have settled down after some experimentation. Initially, the L&SE striped patterns were continued with, and one set of seat covers in the blue stripe pattern was made up for unit 455 5850, one of those painted in NSE livery for the June 1986 launch. The brown striped pattern continued to be installed on first class seats for some time into the NSE era.

The current 'official' NSE moquette patterns are as follows:-
Blue Blaze 1: Light blue and light grey diagonal flicks on a mid-blue background. This is the most common standard class pattern.
Blue Blaze 2: Red and Dark blue flicks on a mid-blue background. Fitted to sliding door stock with low-backed seating, such as classes 313 and 455.
First Class: Similar to Blue Blaze 2, but with much smaller flicks, giving an overall purple appearance.

First class compartments are generally fitted with dark blue curtains, and carpets featuring NSE flashes on a grey background. Carpets are fitted throughout in class 442.

Class 442 Wessex Electrics have a grey and red moquette pattern in first class.

A new development is to concentrate particular standard class upholstery patterns onto particular lines. For example, suburban stock on South London Lines routes is being given Blue Blaze 1 seat covers, while on South Western Lines, Blue Blaze 2 will become the norm.

Ticketing and Railcards

Standard Tickets and Cheap Day Returns Standard tickets are available for travel at any time, single or return. Cheap day returns are valid after 09 30 on weekdays, all day at weekends and Bank Holidays. All are now only valid on the date shown on the ticket. Other than tickets to London BR, through tickets to Zone 1 on London Transport are also available.

Travelcards The One-Day Capitalcard was launched at the same time as NSE, being available from 11th June 1986, and gave off-peak travellers the freedom of London's rail and bus services within an area roughly similar to the old GLC. Customers travelling in from outside this area could purchase a One-Day Capitalcard for only slightly more than the cost of a Day Return to London. Basically the ticket was valid from 09 30 on weekdays and all day at Weekends (including Bank Holidays), but passengers coming in from outside the Capitalcard zones could start earlier depending on the distance out (for example, the first train out of Bognor Regis on which a Capitalcard could be used was the 08 10). The One-Day Capitalcard was an outstanding success, generating £40 million of business in the first year. From 6th January 1989, the One Day Capitalcard was renamed 'One Day Travelcard', as part of a revised revenue agreement with LRT. Monthly sales are now well over one million. Travelcard Season Tickets for periods of one week, one month or annually (see 'Gold Card' below) are available for travel at all times.

Network Card This was launched on 29th September 1986, as the first BR railcard available to *everyone*, regardless of age or status. The card gives up to ⅓ discount on all tickets, but may only be used after 10 00 on weekdays (any time at weekends and Bank Holidays). Up to three other adults may also travel with the holder for the same ⅓ discount, and up to four children may also travel in the party for a flat fare of £1. There are various other benefits of owning one of these cards: in particular holders may currently travel first class for a £3 supplement at weekends. There is often a discount on any 'Gala Day' fare offered.

Network Gold Card During 1987, the former annual season ticket became the Network Gold Card, in recognition of the long-term commitment made to rail travel by holders of such tickets. Apart from being usable as a Network Card (with the same validity) by the holder for optional travel at weekends etc, it also enables him or her to obtain a free Gold Card Partner's Network Card for a friend or relative. Gold Card holders are also sent regular quarterly 'Gold Card News' mailings with details of occasional special selected offers as well as news about the Network. An increasing number of Gold Card holders now have the option of renewing the cards by post.

Network Awaybreak Initially introduced as the Network Saver (the name was changed, together with minor alterations to validity in 1989) this discounted return ticket is available for journeys within the NSE area of more than about 30 miles (40 miles in the London area). Not available for use until after 09 30 on weekdays (after 10 00 if purchased with a Network Card), the holder could return any day up to one month after the date on the ticket. From June 1990, the valid period was reduced to 5 days only, to target it to the short break market for which it was designed.

Ticket Issuing Arrangements: All stations on NSE (and indeed on BR) with a manned ticket office are equipped with 'Aptis' (All-purpose ticket issuing system) computerised ticket issuing machines, which issue credit-card sized tickets. These are all connected to a central computer which makes accounting a far simpler process than previously. A feature of Aptis is that separate outward and return tickets are issued. Tickets issued by Aptis machines (or the self-service machines mentioned below) have a magnetic strip on the rear; in appropriate cases these operate the automatic ticket gates on LRT central area stations. A portable version of Aptis is known as 'Sportis' (developed from an earlier type known as 'Portis'), and these machines may be carried by guards or revenue protection officers on trains.

A recent development is the installation of self-service ticket machines at many stations. They issue the most popular tickets in the same format as Aptis tickets. Until recently they were all located in ticket halls to cut down queues, but they are now also being installed outside stations and on platforms so that intending customers may purchase a ticket even when the booking office is closed, thus providing a 24-hour ticket selling facility. It is planned that such machines, manufactured by the Swiss firm Ascom/Autelca, will be installed at the majority of Network stations in the near future. The machines are very robust and reliability is high, having proved themselves in a number of continental countries.

Ticket Inspection: There is a policy of converting stations from being 'closed' to 'open' in terms of ticket inspection; that is, a change from manned ticket barriers to open entrances and exits. This is partly an exercise to make stations (which are generally the customers' first contact with the railway) more inviting and user friendly and partly to reduce staffing costs. Parts of NSE are now 'open' in terms of stations, with ticket examination carried out on trains. Access to platforms is only officially allowed for persons holding a valid travel ticket or platform ticket. It is policy to have a ticket inspection purge on a major station or line at intervals, when all exits are heavily manned by ticket inspectors. This has been particularly effective in deterring fraudulent travel, and is carried out jointly with Inspectors from London Buses, London Underground and the Docklands Light Railway.

On inner-suburban trains operating on routes with manned stations and with short times between station stops, it is often difficult for trainmen to inspect tickets and collect fares, although this obviously has to be the case on trains calling at unstaffed stations, where a second member of traincrew can issue tickets from a Sportis ticket machine. On outer-suburban and express routes, ticket inspection is undertaken by Conductors, while on the increasing number of Driver Only Operated (DOO) services, inspection (or what has become known as 'revenue protection'), is carried out by Mobile Travelling Ticket Inspectors (TTIs), who may also carry Sportis machines. They obviously have the ability to switch from train to train at, for example, Clapham Junction, to cover a wider area.

It is now policy that intending customers must have a valid ticket before boarding a train, if it is possible. If they do not do so, they are liable to pay the full standard single fare for the journey undertaken, with no railcard or other discounts available. The recent installation of ticket machines outside station premises makes it easier to purchase tickets when booking offices are closed.

BR has now obtained legislation to enable Travelling Ticket Inspectors to charge a penalty fare if a passenger is caught travelling without a ticket or authority to travel (obtained from the special machines installed at stations). Activating orders issued by the Department of Transport are needed for each route, and the system (which has been in use on a number of European Railways for some years) is gradually being introduced. Before coming into effect on any route, the Secretary of State has to be satisfied that all staff have been properly trained in the procedures. The first area in which the system came into force was on London, Tilbury and Southend services out of Fenchurch Street, and this has since been followed by part of the South Western Lines. It is hoped that these measures will be effective in combating fare evasion.

Progress So Far and Future Plans

Electrification: The following lines have been electrified since the formation of Network SouthEast. Those on Southern Region have been electrified on the 750V dc conductor-rail system, those on other regions on the 25kV ac overhead system. Lines on which work had started before June 1986 are denoted by an asterisk and the dates of commencement of individual electric services are shown in brackets:

Wickford - Southminster* (October 1986)
Hitchin - Peterborough* (May 1987)
Bishops Stortford - Cambridge* (May 1987)
Sanderstead - East Grinstead* (October 1987)
Bournemouth - Weymouth* (May 1988)
Watford - St Albans Abbey (August 1988)
Royston - Cambridge (October 1988)
Portsmouth - Southampton/Eastleigh (May 1990)

In progress at present is Cambridge – King's Lynn.

New and Reopened Lines: Under the 'Speller Amendment' to the relevant Act of Parliament, it is possible for BR to reopen lines and stations without going through the customary closure proceedings if the undertaking proves unsuccessful. Under these arrangements, Network SouthEast has experimentally re-opened two lines, both originally closed under Beeching in the 1960s. That from Oxford to Bicester Town, with through running of some trains from Didcot, has proved a success, and a further station has been opened on the line at Islip. That from Kettering to Corby has been less successful after a promising start, and was closed again from June 1990 following withdrawal of local authority financial support.

Thameslink: Following a 1984 joint study by the erstwhile Greater London Council (GLC) and BR, it was decided to reopen the short connection from Blackfriars on Southern Region to Farringdon on the recently modernised and electrified LMR Midland Suburban Line from Bedford to St Pancras and Moorgate. This useful connection had been constructed by the LC&DR in the nineteenth century, but as recounted earlier in the chapter passenger services over it finished in 1916 (though it was not finally closed as a freight route until 1969). Electrified on the standard Southern Region 750V dc system, it was reopened to passenger traffic in May 1988. Titled 'Thameslink', there was a completely recast service of through trains via the new tunnel from stations on the Bedford line to various SR destinations such as Brighton, Sevenoaks and Purley. A fleet of sixty new dual-voltage EMUs, classified 319, was constructed to work the new services, changeover from one electrical system to the other taking place during a slightly extended station stop at Farringdon. For a relatively minor financial outlay, Thameslink has proved extremely successful and from May 1990 a new service was provided from Guildford to Luton. A new station on the link named St Paul's Thameslink, to replace Holborn Viaduct terminus, was also opened at roughly the same time as part of a new City office development. A further twenty-six class 319 units to increase services commenced delivery during the latter part of the year. It seems likely that further improvements to Thameslink will go ahead, and various parts of this are currently awaiting Parliamentary powers. Much will depend on the provision of a new sub-surface station on the King's Cross/St Pancras site, as part of new Channel Tunnel works, replacing the present cramped King's Cross Thameslink station. A connection will be built for through running onto the Great Northern suburban lines, while terminating outer-suburban services from the north will all run into St Pancras. It is hoped to quadruple the present double track between Borough Market and Metropolitan Junctions (currently worked to absolute capacity). These improvements, together with new junctions east of the station making use of already available infrastructure, will enable a much more intensive through service via London Bridge possible.

East-West Crossrail Built to main line loading gauge for NSE and Underground trains, this would connect suburban lines from Paddington and Marylebone and LUL's Metropolitan Line with those from Liverpool Street. It is hoped that work will start on this scheme in 1993.

Heathrow Airport Link Although a link from the Underground's Piccadilly Line to Heathrow Airport was completed in 1977, there has long been a case for a faster route from the World's busiest international airport (currently handling 35 million passengers per annum) into Central London. Following the report of the 1986 'Heathrow Surface Access Study', the Government approved in principle plans for a new surface railway, to branch off from the main NSE Paddington – Reading line near Hayes and Harlington. The line will be jointly promoted by Heathrow Airport Ltd (a wholly-owned subsidiary of BAA) and NSE. HAL will finance and own the new line, including two stations at Heathrow, and will provide customer service staff on the new trains.

Stansted Airport An integral part of the development of Stansted Airport in Essex as London's third airport was the construction of a rail link to the airport, branching off from the Liverpool Street – Cambridge main line between Stansted Mountfichet and Elsenham. Starting with a triangular junction, enabling the operation of train services from both north and south, construction work on the new link was commenced in 1987. The central section of the route is in single-track tunnel under the main runway, and an important stage was reached with the breakthrough of this tunnel in 1989. The new line is electrified on the standard 25kV ac overhead system, and is financed entirely by NSE. Construction was due to be completed early in 1991, and a half-hourly shuttle to and from Liverpool Street was planned to commence in May of that year, using dedicated rolling stock (class 322) and calling only at Tottenham Hale for interchange with the London Underground Victoria Line.

New and Rebuilt Stations An impressive number of stations has been built or reopened since the formation of Network SouthEast in 1986, and these are listed in the Stations chapter. In addition more than 60 stations have been totally reconstructed, and nearly 250 modernised. An on-going programme of station painting had covered more than one-third of the Network in the first four years. Much more attention is now being paid to keeping even the most outlying stations clean, and the yellow 'Station Cleaning Team' vans are becoming a familiar sight in NSE station car parks.

New Rolling Stock The following new trains (all electric multiple units, reflecting the predominance of electrified lines and the ongoing electrification programme on NSE) entered service between 1986 and early 1990:

20 x class 317/2 four-car units for Great Northern outer-suburban services. (These were actually in the course of delivery in June 1986, and the first were the last to be outshopped new in blue/grey).

24 x class 442 five-car express units for Waterloo - Bournemouth - Weymouth fast services.

60 x class 319 four-car units for through Thameslink services from Bedford to Brighton etc, commencing in May 1988.

114 x class 321 four-car units for Great Eastern, West Anglia and Northampton Line services.

The following stock is due for delivery during the currency of this publication:

5 x class 322 four-car units for the dedicated Liverpool Street - Stansted Airport shuttle, due to commence in May 1991.

26 x class 319 four-car units to augment Thameslink services.

24 x class 456 two-car units for South London Lines services.

180 x class 165 'Network Turbo' DMU vehicles, for Chiltern (89 coaches) and Thames (91 coaches) lines.

5 x class 482 four-car units for the Waterloo and City line.

A wooden mock-up showing how the cab-front of the Kent Link 'Networker' would appear, on display to commuters at Charing Cross on 12th December 1989. Note in particular the large dot-matrix headcode and destination display — hopefully this latter information will also be included inside the train. Brian Morrison

Rolling Stock

With its large mileage of electrified lines, it is not surprising that when Network SouthEast came into being on 10th June 1986, the majority of stock inherited was of the Electric Multiple Unit (EMU) type. Unfortunately, much of it was (and remains) of very out-dated design. A much smaller number of Diesel Multiple Units with either electric (DEMU) or mechanical (DMMU) transmissions was also in use on non-electrified routes, while locomotives and hauled coaching stock were utilised on a number of longer-distance services. Although virtually all the electric unit classes were unique to NSE, the other types, such as class 47/4 diesel-electric locomotives and class 101 DMMUs, were parts of larger fleets with other members allocated to other BR sectors. Since the formation of NSE, investment in new EMUs has resulted in the average age of the fleet dropping from 25 to 21 years, and it is hoped to reduce the amount of loco-hauled working, which is less efficient, substantially over the next few years. With electrification schemes steadily being implemented also, the amount of diesel stock in use will likewise drop substantially. However, on routes where electrification will not take place, new 'Network Turbo' diesel units will be introduced; the first fleet has already been ordered for the Chiltern and Thames Valley lines out of Marylebone and Paddington.

Pre-war, the most developed parts of the London suburban railway network were those of the Southern Railway (SR), and the Great Eastern area of the London and North Eastern Railway (LNER). As recounted in an earlier chapter, the SR had had an ongoing programme of electrification on the third-rail 660V DC system since 1914, and therefore possessed by far the most experience in EMU design and operation. For this reason, Southern stock influenced the design of trains built for the 1955 Modernisation Plan electrifications. SR suburban stock had a 6-a-side seating (or 5 with a central gangway) with traditional slam-doors to each seating bay, a layout which dated almost from the earliest days of railways.

Although the GE suburban lines were as busy as those of the SR, the LNER fought shy of electrification due to the expense until the late 1930s, when the first stage was started, financed by cheap Government loans, between Liverpool Street and Shenfield. For this scheme (not completed until 1949 due to a hold-up caused by World War 2) sliding-door EMUs with bright modern interiors were constructed. It is a shame that BR designers did not take more notice of these when contemplating their new trains, or of a similar projected (but never built) LMS design for their London-area lines. Instead, dated, draughty and drab SR-type designs (some of them in fact built at the SR workshops at Eastleigh) were perpetuated for suburban and outer-suburban lines out of Liverpool Street and Fenchurch Street, as well as on new stock for the Southern Region and elsewhere. Thus, the erstwhile class 306 units remained the only sliding-door units in London (apart from the 'Pep' prototypes) until 1976, when the class 313s started being delivered for the Great Northern inner-suburban electrification. The 306s were withdrawn in 1981; happily one remains in working order at Ilford Depot for apprentice training.

In fairness, it should be said that the SR slam-door layout does give the maximum number of seats in a given vehicle length, as well as speedy loading and unloading at stations. It was also cheaper than sliding door stock to build, an important consideration given the number of new vehicles required. However, the fact remains that it is extremely outdated, and unsuited to modern-day operating conditions, such as driver-only operation (DOO).

Main-line units for the SR electrified routes to the South Coast and Kent built between 1956 and 1974 were equally uninspiring, still being based on Mark 1 bodyshells. Earlier units (class 411 '4 Cep') were firmly based on pre-War types, while later designs (class 421 '4 Cig' and class 423 '4 Vep') were extremely out-of-date by the time the last rolled off the production line in 1974. The only other main line electric units built, the class 309 'Clacton' units were similar, but at least they looked the part more, with stylish wrap-around cab windows that have unfortunately since been replaced. Most of these types will need to remain in service for many more years, and many have been rebuilt with modern interiors.

Diesel Multiple Units were also introduced as part of the 1955 modernisation scheme, to replace steam haulage on non-electrified routes. Those built for the Southern Region were DEMUs of rather specialised design; they were similar to electric units but had above-floor mounted diesel engines powering virtually standard SR electric traction equipment. The best known of these were the special narrow-bodied express units for the Charing Cross-Tonbridge-Hastings line, mostly withdrawn when the route was electrified in 1986. On other Regions, diesel mechanical units (DMMUs) with underfloor-mounted engines and gearboxes were universal. Those specially built for suburban routes around London (and other major conurbations such as Birmingham and Glasgow) again had bodyshells based on the SR EMU model, with side doors to each seating bay and 2+3 seating with central gangway. Such types still remain on Thames and Chiltern services, while others have been displaced by electrification in recent years. Other DMMU classes such as 101 and 119 have generally been drafted into the area more recently; they have fewer doors and are more suited to rural branch line (such as Colchester-Sudbury) or cross-country (such as Reading-Gatwick) workings.

ELECTRIC MULTIPLE UNITS

An electric multiple unit comprises a number of vehicles (2,3,4,5 and 6 car types work on NSE) permanently coupled together, with a driving cab at each end. One or more vehicles within the unit have motors. Two or more units may be coupled together to make a longer train when required. The length of train which may run on a particular route depends on a number of factors, such as station platform length and power supply. The longest EMU formations which run on NSE are of 12 coaches.

Bodywork

The most obvious design feature of a train is its bodywork. As far as NSE EMUs are concerned, there are seven major design types currently in service or on order.

(a) Southern Region 'Bulleid' type. These have all-steel welded bodies on separate underframes, many of which were recovered from pre-War EMUs. They are distinguished by an even curvature of the side and characteristic lozenge-shaped windows above the droplights on the doors. All are purely suburban.
Classes 415/1, 415/4, 415/5 and 416/3.

(b) British Railways Mark 1 type. These form easily the largest group, and again have all-steel welded bodies on separate underframes. The suburban types look superficially similar to the SR design, but have slightly different body profile and no 'lozenges' on the doors. The main-line types generally have fewer doors but possess gangwayed cab ends. There are many differences in front end, window design etc between various classes to this design.
Suburban and Outer Suburban: Classes 302, 305, 308, 413, 414, 415/6, 416/1, 416/4.
Main Line: Classes 309, 411, 412, 421, 422, 423, 431.

(c) British Railways Mark 2 Type. These have integral bodies without separate underframes, but retain slam-doors. They have an almost straight profile which curves inwards sharply near the bottom. All NSE ones now work on outer-suburban duties on Anglia Region.
Classes 310, 312.

(d) Aluminium-Bodied Sliding Door Type. Again of integral construction, these have a similar profile to the Mark-2 type, but with a lower roof line. They possess two pairs of sliding doors on the side of each vehicle, large windows with 'hopper' type ventilators, and a front end with a recessed central emergency door. All are used for suburban services.
Classes 313, 315. (One trailer vehicle in each Class 455/7 unit is also of this type).

(e) Steel-Bodied Mark 3-derived Sliding Door Type. This is the standard BREL EMU design for the 1980s, and was still in production at the beginning of the 1990s. The basic layout is similar to the aluminium-bodied stock described above, but the roof is higher and has characteristic longitudinal raised strips along it. Various front end designs have been tried on successive types, with or without a gangway or emergency door, and various interior layouts make the units suitable for suburban and outer-suburban use.
Suburban: Classes 455, 456
Outer Suburban: Classes 317, 319, 321, 322

(f) Mark 3 Type. These are a variant of the Mark 3 loco-hauled and HST main line vehicles, but have plug doors and a distinctive gangwayed cab end with wrap-around windows.
Class 442.

(g) 'Networker'. As a 'concept train', current plans for this stock are detailed later.

Traction Equipment

Further details of the electrification systems in the NSE area will be found in the 'Electrification Systems' chapter, but briefly are now of two types:

(a) 750 Volts Direct Current (DC), collected from a conductor rail (or 'third rail') mounted just outside the running rails, via pick-up shoes which slide along the top of the conductor rail.

(b) 25000 Volts Alternating Current (AC) collected from an overhead wire via a sprung pantograph.

Most locomotives and units are equipped for working off one system or the other, but EMUs of classes 313 and 319 will work off both. AC and dual-voltage EMUs have class numbers in the 3xx series, while DC stock is classed in the 4xx series.

The electrical equipment in DC stock is somewhat simpler, so will be described first. This is virtually all SR stock, and fittings are highly standardised for economy and ease of maintenance. EMUs generally (with a few exceptions) have one motor bogie per pair of coaches, each equipped with two axle-hung traction motors. Earlier stock (classes 411, 412, 413, 414, 415 and 416) generally has a motor bogie under the driving cab at each end of a 4-car unit, but on more recent stock the motor bogies are concentrated under one intermediate vehicle. The EE507 traction motor, introduced in 1950 and produced (or reconditioned) in several versions since, is all but standard, being rated variously at 250 or 275hp. It is interesting to note that many 455 units, introduced from 1983, are powered by rebuilt (to metric standards!) motors dating from the 1950s. The speed of the train is controlled by varying the current available to the motors, generally by diverting it through banks of underframe-mounted resistors which are gradually switched out or reconnected in different electrical configurations as the train accelerates. In normal running, this is all done automatically through switches operated electro-pneumatically ('1951 stock' in SR operating jargon), or by hydraulic camshaft ('1957 stock' and later). This system is standard on all SR stock up to class 442. Current collector shoes are generally mounted on the end bogies of each unit (class 442 has some situated intermediately as well).

With developments in power electronics and the advent of micro-processor control systems, thyristor or 'chopper' control has been used in the most modern EMUs. The thyristor takes power in 'chunks' and smooths it out before it reaches the motors. Apart from anything else, this system takes up far less space, doing away with the vast banks of resistors on motor-coach underframes. The last five production 455s were fitted with this system when built, and a more advanced version equips the class 319 dual-voltage 'Thameslink' trains.

Following early experiments with AC traction motors, it was discovered (by the French, probably leaders in AC traction technology at the time) that the easiest way to power a train by AC current was to transform and rectify it on the train for use by DC equipment. General comments above regarding distribution of motors etc also apply here. Early examples of AC EMUs and locomotives built for Modernisation Plan electrification schemes in the 1950s had mercury arc rectifiers, but the functioning of these was not helped by splashing mercury as the train bounced along. Much more satisfactory on-train rectifiers followed the development of solid-state silicon and germanium-diode devices, and these are now standard on older stock (classes 302-313). Traction motors are nothing like as standardised as on DC stock, AC units being equipped variously by English Electric, GEC (the former's successor) and Brush. Units of classes 313 and 315 have two motor coaches each with two motor bogies carrying two lower powered motors, but more recent builds (classes 317 upwards) revert to an immediate power car with two higher-powered motor bogies. The pantograph is usually mounted at one end of the motor coach roof (over the brake van if there is one), or in the case of classes 313 and 315 over an intermediate trailer.

Brakes and Running Gear

The Southern Region introduced electro-pneumatic brakes in its 'EPB' stock of 1951, together with automatic 'buckeye' couplings at unit ends. The brakes were coupled between units by waist-level hoses, which could be easily disconnected or connected by staff at platform level. This same basic system was used for all SR stock up to the class 442 'Wessex Electric' (with the exception of the class 508 and 455 sliding-door suburban units, the former soon banished to Merseyside and therefore outside the scope of this book), and thus almost any SR EMU can couple and work with almost any other, subject to various restrictions. The units concerned often have the letters 'EP' in their SR classification. Thus, suburban class 416/3 '2 EPB' units work with main line class 423 '4 Vep' units on East Grinstead line services etc.

The same basic system was utilised in the AC stock built in the 1950s and 1960s, and similar compatibility applies. The author remembers seeing an odd cavalcade formed of classes 308, 312 and 309 on a Saturday Liverpool Street to Walton-on-the-Naze train a few summers ago.

Modern sliding-door stock is fitted with the 'Westcode' EP brake, which is controlled electrically without any physical pneumatic connection between units when coupled. This facilitates the use of fully-automatic couplers, with brake and multiple-unit control connections built in, but seems to have taken drivers a long time to get used to! After experience with the class 508 units (similar to class 315, but now transferred to Liverpool) however, the Southern Region fought shy of these couplings on its new stock, so the class 455s retain jumper cables which have to be attached or detached separately. The modern coupling is known as the 'Tightlock'; unlike the equivalent 'Wedgelock' coupler used on London Underground stock it is not 'handed' so individual EMUs may be coupled to each other facing either direction.

As far as bogies are concerned, there are many and varied designs. The oldest (under SR suburban stock) has leaf primary springing. The 'Commonwealth' bogie was introduced on various express units (the 'Clacton' class 309s and later Kent Coast '4 Cep's) during the late 1950s in an attempt to cure the rough-riding to which high-speed EMUs seem particularly prone; this has a heavy cast-metal frame and coil springing. New units built for the Great Eastern electrification schemes were generally fitted with 'Gresley' bogies, developed from a type designed by the LNER CME before WW2. Motor bogies were generally of heavier construction than trailer bogies, carrying as they did the traction motors and gearing. New bogie types were developed in the 1960s, being fitted under SR stock introduced between 1964-74, the LMR class 310s and ER class 312s. Known as 'B4', 'B5' and 'B5S', they had fabricated frames and coil springing; the SR 'B5S' type had additional external dampers. These bogies have also been fitted under older refurbished stock, particularly on Anglia Region, but in this case they were recovered from withdrawn locomotive-hauled stock.

A number of experimental bogie types were fitted under the experimental 'Pep' prototype train (really the forerunner of today's sliding door stock), and the most successful designs have been utilised under all new EMU stock built for the NSE area since the 313s of 1976. These (classified BX1, BP13 and BP20) have air-bag secondary suspension between the bogie and vehicle body. Following problems with the early class 317s, which regularly work at 100mph, additional dampers are fitted to all stock which operates at 90-100mph, but the SR 455s do not need them, being limited to 75mph. These latest bogie types (and the B4s under 310/312s) are generally equipped with disc brakes, earlier types having clasp brakes. An unfortunate fault of these disc brakes (also known to passengers on InterCity services worked by HSTs) is the unpleasant smell emanating from them – new disc materials are helping to eradicate this.

Interior Design

The majority of stock is of the 'Open' or 'Saloon' type, with seats either side of a central gangway. In suburban and outer-suburban stock, there are three seats on one side of the gangway and two on the other, henceforth referred to as '3+2'. In express stock, the seating is generally two each side of the gangway, or '2+2'. In older stock (of Mark 1 and Mark 2 design) the seats are arranged in bays and face each other, but in more modern sliding-door stock, there is some 'face-to-back' or unidirectional seating, which can be squeezed in slighty more tightly. All SR express units have the odd standard class compartment also, seating three (classes 411 and 412) or four each side.

In those units which have first class accommodation, this is either arranged in compartments seating three each side with a side gangway (SR stock and class 309) or open in a 2+2 arrangement.

The traditional SR seat design had a high back with headrest, with the luggage rack conveniently perched above. This was perpetuated in BR Mark 1 and Mark 2 stock, although outer-suburban and express types often had longitudinal racks above the windows. Armrests were often affixed to the seats or the coach sides in standard class, with intermediate folding armrests also in first class.

Low-backed seats with separate cushions or 'squabs' with removable covers (which could therefore be easily cleaned) were first introduced in the class 313 sliding-door stock of 1976, and are standard on modern inner-suburban stock. A more comfortable version with high back and separate headrest was used in the outer-suburban class 317 units, and was also fitted to rebuilt units of classes 302, 305 and 308. It has been found that these headrests are prone to fall (or be pulled) off. A newer design with one-piece high-back has been used in classes 319 and 321, and this is being retro-fitted to class 317.

The Kent Coast express stock of classes 411 and 412 was rebuilt with modern interiors featuring 2+2 seating of 'InterCity 70' design, with removable covers and solid non-folding armrests. Comments about headrests falling off apply here also. The Clacton class 309 units were rebuilt similarly, but with rather more spartan seating with one-piece backs and small folding armrests at the outer seat ends only. The most recent express stock, the 'Wessex Electrics' class 442s, have seats of a new design, similar in both first and standard class. The first class seats in the second batch of 321s are also of this type.

Early stock generally had laminate or wood panelling, often in rather dreary tones accentuated by shadowy lighting from bare bulbs. New and refurbished stock generally features panelling in white or light shades of grey, brightly illuminated by fluorescent tubes. Some units have moulded fibreglass window-surrounds, sliding door pockets etc, but these are often a poor fit. The early class 317s and 455s are particularly bad, but more recent builds have been somewhat better, although still often spoiled by low-cost fittings which look tacky and quickly get broken.

New stock is invariably equipped with a public address system, enabling the crew to speak to each other and to passengers. Earlier stock which has been 'facelifted' or refurbished also has this feature.

For details of upholstery fabric patterns, interior maps etc, refer to the section on 'The Network Image' in chapter 1.

The salient features of the various classes will now be described in more detail, in numerical class order.

Class 302

Fleet Size: Approx. 50 units, of which 30 have been refurbished.
Formation (refurbished units): Driving Trailer Composite +
Motor Brake Standard + Trailer Standard + Driving Trailer Standard.
Traction Equipment: 4 × EE 536A.
Maximum Speed: 75mph
Present Sphere of Operation: London, Tilbury and Southend; Great Eastern.

This fleet of EMUs was built in 1958-59 for the newly electrified lines out of Fenchurch Street. Although constructed at York and Doncaster, they were very much of 'Southern' style, having suburban Mark 1 bodies without gangways, a very functional upright cab end (but with rather larger windscreens than the SR design), a side door to each seating bay and standard class seating in a mixture of 3+2 with centre gangway and non-corridor 6-a-side compartments. Unlike contemporary SR designs, they had one intermediate motor coach, and all trailing (non-motored) bogies were of the Gresley type.

Thirty units have been fully refurbished in the same manner as classes 305, 307 and 308 (see below), and these can be recognised externally by a blanked-off headcode panel, headlamps and alloy window surrounds. First class accommodation is moved to a new saloon directly behind the cab in the DTC, and the interiors are completely new, with 317 style seating with removable covers, new panelling and fluorescent strip lighting. Gangways have been fitted between vehicles in each unit, and the original bogies have been replaced by newer B4 or B5 coil-sprung types. Most presently retain blue/grey livery, although a few carry NSE stripes.

Rebuilt class 302 EMU 302209 stands in the dusk at Upminster on 16th December 1989, leading the 15.42 Fenchurch Street-Shoeburyness. This particular unit remains in blue/grey livery, and the flat front, which distinguishes the type from otherwise similar class 305 and 308, may be noted. As is common on London, Tilbury and Southend line services, no destination blind is carried. Chris Wilson

Class 305/1

Fleet Size: 22 units.
Number Series: 305 401-422
Formation: Driving Trailer Standard +
Non-Driving Motor Brake Standard + Driving Trailer Standard.
Traction Equipment: 4 × GEC WT380
Maximum Speed: 75mph
Present Sphere of Operation: West Anglia (see text).

This small class is what remains of a much larger series built for the 1960 electrification of the inner suburban lines from Liverpool Street to Enfield, Chingford and Hertford East. Although built to the Mark 1 suburban design with similar features to classes 302 etc, they had a new-style cab front designed at Wolverton, with sloping cab windows, a domed roof and rounded corners. Other features were large windows between the doors and attractive low-backed seating, suitable for the short-distance services they were designed for. Although remaining on the routes for which they were built, they generally only appear in the peaks, most of their workings having been taken over by class 315. Most have had a minor facelift, and all retain blue/grey livery.

Class 305/2 & 305/3

Fleet Size: 25 Units
Number Series: 305 501-511, 513-519, 521-528
Formation: Driving Trailer Composite + Motor Brake Standard +
Trailer Standard + Driving Trailer Standard (see text).
Traction Equipment: 4 × GEC WT 380
Maximum Speed: 75mph
Present Sphere of Operation: Anglia Electrics; London, Tilbury and Southend.

Again built in 1960, this time for outer-suburban services out of Liverpool Street, 305 501-519 have now all been refurbished in a similar fashion to class 302, and are now all-but identical in accommodation, other than being non-gangwayed. They have the 'Wolverton' cab end, however, and retain their Gresley bogies.

A further series was created in 1988-89 by reforming otherwise redundant class 305/1 units with a trailer composite from a withdrawn class 302. All vehicles have been completely rebuilt internally, with modern high-backed 319 style seating. Surprisingly, all have been outshopped in the old blue/grey livery. This sub-class works solely on the LT&S, and may easily be distinguished because the ex-305/1 vehicles retain their large side windows.

Class 308/1

Fleet Size: 33 × 4-car units.
Number Series: 308 133-165
Formation: See class 305/2.
Traction Equipment: 4 × English Electric 536A.
Maximum Speed: 75mph
Present Sphere of Operation: London, Tilbury and Southend.

Virtually identical to the 'original' rebuilt class 305/2 EMUs, these units have English Electric rather than GEC traction equipment.

Left The class 308/1 units have all been rebuilt and work exclusively on London, Tilbury and Southend line services. In spite of the destination blind, 308149 is actually heading away from Fenchurch Street in this photograph, as it passes Shadwell in January 1990. Alex Dasi-Sutton

Class 309

Fleet Size: 23 × 4-car units.
Number Series: 309 601-608, 309 611-627.
Formation: Driving Motor Brake Standard + Trailer Standard +
Trailer Composite + Driving Trailer Standard (309/1)
or Driving Trailer Composite + Motor Brake Standard +
Trailer Standard + Driving Trailer Standard (309/2).
Traction Equipment: 4 × GEC WT401
Maximum Speed: 100mph
Present Sphere of Operation: Great Eastern (Liverpool Street-Clacton/Walton/
Harwich/Norwich)

The class 309s were introduced in 1962-63, and were intended to be the first of a fleet of express EMUs for use on the AC electrified lines, but in the event remained a small class. Notable as being the first 100mph EMUs on BR, they were largely based on the SR '4 Cep's, having express-type mark 1 bodyshells and very comfortable 2+2 standard class seating. They featured attractive wrap-around windscreens (replaced by flat glass in the mid-1970s, a change which somewhat spoilt their appearance) and when built were the only electric units to sport the maroon coach livery rather than green.

Originally there were three types of unit: 4-car with or without a buffet 'griddle' car, and 2-car. The buffet cars were withdrawn in 1978 and the 2-car units made up to 4 cars, utilising modified ex-loco hauled mark 1 vehicles. The fleet went through a refurbishment at Wolverton Works between 1985 and 1987, the first few being outshopped in L&SE 'jaffa-cake' livery, and branded 'Essex Express'. By utilising more ex-hauled stock, it was possible to rationalise the class into two types, both roughly equivalent in seating capacity. The refurbishment involved the provision of new seating in standard class, strip lighting and 'hopper' ventilated windows. The class is now all in NSE livery, and as well as working the Liverpool Street-Clacton fast trains, also works to Harwich (including some boat trains) and Norwich. The units are not suitable for services involving frequent stopping and starting, as this tends to overheat their resistors.

Class 310 and 312

Fleet Size: 38 × 4-car units (310), 49 × 4-car units (312).
Number Series: 310 001-095, 312 701-730, 312 781-799.
Formation: Battery Driving Trailer Standard + Motor Brake Standard +
Trailer Standard + Driving Trailer Composite
Traction Equipment: 4 × EE546
Maximum Speeds: Class 310 75mph, Class 312 90mph.
Present Sphere of Operation: Great Eastern; West Anglia; London, Tilbury and Southend.

These two classes are the only multiple unit types based on the Mark 2 integral bodyshell on BR. Class 310 are the 'excellent' trains referred to in the electrification section: they were built between 1965 and 1967 for outer suburban services out of Euston. Peculiarly, they are geared for 75mph operation. They have 3+2 seating in standard class and 2+2 in first; in concept at least they are an AC version of the SR's ubiquitous class 423 '4 Vep' units. They were displaced from Northampton Line services in 1988 by class 317s (themselves displaced from the 'Bedpan' line), and were sent to join similar class 312 units on services in Essex. Most have now been refurbished with new laminate interior panelling and a gangway (previously lacking) between the two centre vehicles. Externally, the stylish (but expensive to maintain) wrap-around cab windscreens have been replaced by flat (but toughened) glass – this gives them an appearance all but identical to class 312.

Left **The class 309 units were the first EMUs on BR to be officially capable of 100mph, and were built for the Liverpool Street—Clacton-on-Sea express services. Now extensively rebuilt with new interiors and windows with 'hopper' ventilators, 309612 looks very smart in Network livery, and is seen passing Ilford with an outward working. Right Interior of rebuilt class 309 standard class saloon, showing the new seating. The removable seat covers are in the now-superseded London and South East Sector 'blue stripe' pattern.** NSE

All of class 312 now operate on Great Eastern lines and 312794, seen at Ilford in June 1990, is one of those built for these services. R.C. Riley

Based on the same design, various batches of class 312 were constructed between 1975 and 1978 for the Great Eastern and Great Northern lines. Apart from being geared for 90mph operation, they differ from their older sisters in having flat glass windscreens from new, gangways through the whole unit and only two (rather than four) toilets. Those built for the GE (now 312781-312799) are equipped to operate off 6.25kV as well as 25kV ac: as discussed earlier, this facility is no longer required. The last of the GN units was displaced from the King's Cross lines in 1988. Many of this class have also been refurbished internally.

33

Class 313

Fleet Size: 64 × 3-car units.
Number Series: 313 001-064.
Formation: Motor Standard + Trailer Standard + Motor Standard.
Traction Equipment: 8 × GEC G31OAZ
Maximum Speed: 75mph
Present Sphere of Operation: North London Lines; Great Northern.

Originally constructed for inner-suburban services on the 1976-78 Great Northern Suburban electrification, these were the first production units with aluminium bodyshells based on the 'Pep' prototypes. They were also the first EMUs on BR equipped to work off both 25kV ac overhead and 750V dc third-rail, this latter capability being required to work over the Drayton Park-Moorgate section, tunnel clearances being insufficient for installation of overhead catenary. The traction equipment is fairly conventional however, with camshaft control of DC current to the motors. Another novel feature was the use of fully-automatic 'Tightlock' couplings, for the first time incorporating all air and electrical connections. Initially fitted with a rather peculiar form of passenger-controlled sliding doors, this system was soon abandoned in favour of guard control, and more recently (as DOO has come into force) driver control. Internally, the 3+2 seating is low-backed with removable covers, setting a standard for large numbers of suburban EMUs built subsequently. Since 1987, these units have been used on weekdays only on Great Northern services; at weekends all trains run into King's Cross and 317s are used on the inner- as well as the outer-suburban services.

Facing Page **Working on the route for which these dual-voltage EMUs were constructed, class 313s 313036 and 313059 run into Alexandra Palace with the 17.50 Moorgate—Welwyn Garden City stopping service in August 1989. This was the first production BR-designed sliding door stock introduced in the London area. Twenty-four units of this class are fitted with additional shoegear for working over 'North London Lines' third-rail routes.** Chris Wilson

Since 1985, 313s have worked services from Euston on the Watford 'new' line, electrified at 750V dc third rail. For this the first 17 have been fitted with extra current collector shoes on the outer bogies: these were found to be needed due to the 'gap' configuration state of the third rail on the route. They also replaced very tatty SR 'EPB's on Richmond-North Woolwich services from October 1989, and were also utilised on the Watford Junction-St Albans Abbey route. For these duties further units were given the extra collector shoes, all those so fitted now being based at Bletchley Depot.

Class 315
Fleet Size: 64 × 4-car units.
Number Series: 315 801-861
Formation: Motor Standard + Trailer Standard +
Pantograph Trailer Standard + Motor Standard
Traction Equipment: 8 × Brush TM61-53 or GEC G310BZ
Maximum Speed: 75mph
Present Sphere of Operation: Great Eastern (inner suburban); West Anglia

The largest fleet of EMUs built with the aluminium sliding-door type bodyshell, class 315 was introduced onto Eastern (now Anglia) Region inner-suburban lines out of Liverpool Street from 1980, where they replaced the venerable class 306 'Shenfield' EMUs. They are generally similar to class 313, but work off 25kV only, have more advanced thyristor control equipment, and passenger-operated sliding doors with interior and exterior push-buttons. When first introduced, these units had a bad reputation for reliability, but most faults seem to have been ironed out now.

Originally used on the intensive Gidea Park and Shenfield stopping service, their use was extended for a time to include Southend line trains (for which they were not particularly suitable, having neither first class nor toilets). More recently, some have been transferred to North East Essex inner-suburban lines, working as far up as Hertford East. Virtually all are now in NSE colours, which suits these modern-looking trains well.

Class 317
Fleet Size: 72 × 4-car units
Number Series: 317 301-372
Formation: Driving Trailer Standard + Motor Standard +
Trailer Composite + Driving Trailer Standard
Traction Equipment: 4 × GEC G315BZ
Maximum Speed: 100mph
Present Sphere of Operation: Great Northern; Thameslink*; West Anglia.

These were the first production EMUs (after the '210' diesel-electric MU prototypes) to make use of the mark 3 'suburban' bodyshell, which superseded the aluminium one because of its lower cost. The first batch of 48 were built at York in 1981-82 for the Midland Suburban electrification, but remained out-of-use in sidings until mid-1983, pending the resolution of a union dispute involving driver-only operation (DOO), which these units introduced on BR. Entry into service brought to light several serious design faults, but these were soon rectified to give NSE one of its most reliable EMU fleets.

Seconded back to rush hour services on the Bedford line until the new class 319/1s were delivered in the latter half of 1990, class 317/1 No.317323 stands at Kings Cross Thameslink on 4th January 1990, forming the 18.20 Moorgate—St Albans. Originally built for the electrification of this line in 1981, these units now mainly work on 'Great Northern' outer-suburban services. Chris Wilson

It must be stated that these units are not pretty! The standard Mark 3 bodyshell was given a cab end of most peculiar appearance, while the side windows were given odd 'letter box' hopper ventilators which did not fit into the design at all. Internally, they have been described as being designed by 'a colour-blind metal-worker with a grudge' – again the various parts did not seem to fit together, either physically or aesthetically. The ceilings were lifted straight out of main-line Mark 3 vehicles' design, with concealed transverse fluorescent tubes. The 2+2 first class section was fitted in the centre trailer, but this was down-classed before the units finally entered service.

Technically, the class was fitted with GEC thyristor control similar to that on 315s, but there was a reversion to one centrally located motor coach with two motor bogies. BP20 and BP13 bogies with air-bag primary suspension were fitted, but continuous 100mph running revealed weaknesses in the riding qualities, and additional lateral dampers were quickly fitted.

After settling down to reliable service on the 'Bedpan' line, these sprightly 100mph units were displaced by 319s with introduction of 'Thameslink' in 1988. They were overhauled at Eastleigh and Wolverton Works, where the first class accommodation was reinstated and a 'convertible' lockable luggage area was added in one DTS. The fleet was split between the Great Northern and Northampton lines, but has gradually all gone to the former.

Twenty-four further units of class 317/2 were delivered between 1985 and 1987 for use on the Great Northern, in connection with introduction of DOO on the route from King's Cross to Royston (and later Cambridge and Peterborough). They feature the same redesigned front end as on classes 455/7 and 455/9, properly-designed side windows and a continuous rainstrip along each coach. Internally, however, they are almost identical to class 317/1, but have no forced-air ventilation from ceiling fans.

The whole '317' fleet is presently going through an interior renovation programme, the main alteration being the fitting of one-piece backs to the standard class seating.

Class 319 No.319052 is seen at Kentish Town when brand new, pausing with the 16.50 St Albans—Moorgate service on 2nd August 1988. The 'B' Driving Trailer is leading; this has a convertible area with folding seats behind the cab, which may be locked when carrying mail etc. A similar arrangement may be found on class 321, and has been retrospectively fitted on 317s. Chris Wilson

Class 319

Fleet Size: 86 × 4-car units
Number Series: 319 001-060 (319/0), 319 161-186 (319/1)
Formation: Driving Trailer Standard + Non Driving Motor Standard + Trailer Standard + Driving Trailer Standard
Traction Equipment: 4 × GEC G315BZ
Maximum Speed: 100mph
Present Sphere of Operation: Thameslink

These EMUs were built for the reopening of the 'Snow Hill' tunnel connecting the SR at Blackfriars with the LMR route to Bedford. Based on the mark 3 suburban bodyshell, they are basically a 'cleaned up' version of the class 317 (which they displaced on the Bedford line), but have a dual-voltage capability to run on both the SR 750v DC lines and 25kV on the LMR. They were the first production EMUs in service on BR to have GTO thyristor control gear, supplied by GEC, giving savings in both space and energy over conventional camshaft control. Changeover from one system to the other takes place during a slightly extended station stop at Farringdon. 100mph is possible on the AC lines; on the SR they are officially limited to 90mph,

Class 319s were the first new EMUs to be designed after the formation of NSE, and show improvements in interior design and styling over previous stock. The seats have high one-piece backs (no separate headrests to fall off). No litter bins and few trinket trays were visible when they first entered service, but both have been added since, being very necessary in view of the trolley refreshment service offered on the through Brighton/Gatwick Airport-Bedford trains. The interior panelling is in muted grey shades, with yellow around the door vestibules. The doors themselves have bleepers or 'hustle alarms' which sound when they are about to close. End bulkheads display stylised views of landmarks along the route, such as St Pauls Cathedral, by the artist Edward Pond. The saloon behind the cab in the 'B' Driving Trailer has fold-up seats and can be locked up for the carriage of parcels and mail.

Newly delivered class 319/1 dual voltage EMU No.319162 stands inside Selhurst inspection shed prior to commissioning. The main differences when compared to class 319/0 are the GRP 'skirt' under the cab front, a small first class section (nearest the camera in this view) and the latest variation of NSE livery with light grey. David Brown

The cab ends are of a new and rather tidier design, with no proper gangway but a central emergency door. The cab is accessed directly by sliding plug doors, there being no separate vestibule behind. The units are equipped for DOO on both the Bedford line (the equipment was partly recovered from 317s) and the SR South London Lines – thus the cab has two radio receivers.

As recounted in chapter 1, 'Thameslink' has proved extremely successful and 26 further units of the class were ordered for delivery in the latter half of 1990. These form class 319/1 and are numbered from 319 161 upwards. The main difference is that they include first class accommodation, particularly for use on Brighton line commuter trains, where the lack of such seats has been cause for complaint. They also have other detail improvements found on the 321s (see below).

West Anglia class 321 25kV EMU 321341 pulls out of Broxbourne with a Cambridge to Liverpool Street semi-fast service in August 1990. David Brown

Class 321

Fleet Size: 114 × 4-car units
Number Series: 321 301-366, 401-448
Formation: Driving Trailer Composite + Motor Standard +
Trailer Standard + Driving Trailer Standard
Traction Equipment: 4 × Brush TM 2141B
Maximum Speed: 100mph
Present Sphere of Operation: Great Eastern; West Anglia ('321/3'); Northampton Line ('321/4')

Clearly based firmly on the 319s, which they resemble closely both externally and internally, this class of EMUs has replaced (either directly or by cascade) the worst of the slam door stock of classes 302-308 on Anglia Region. They are 25kV only, and have Brush traction equipment. A redesigned front end (which seems to owe much to both current SNCF EMU and Ford car design!) has two large windows but no emergency door, and a sensible-sized electronic dot matrix destination and headcode display. There are various other minor changes to the bodyshell behind the cabs. Livery now incorporates the lighter grey shade first used on the 'Wessex' class 442s.

Internally, the door vestibules are now grey, and the ambience is rather murky. The class 321/3 units for Anglia services to Southend and Cambridge were built with a rather derisory first class section behind the cab in the 'A' Driving Trailer but this has been improved. First class has also been expanded in the Northampton Line 321/4s, with better seating, and these are to be retro-fitted to the earlier units. The standard class seating in these later units is also more widely spaced.

Class 322

Fleet Size: 5 × 4-car units
Number Series: 322 481-485.
Most details are identical to class 321, but see text.

Class 322 is a modified version of class 321 for operating the half-hourly London Liverpool Street-Stansted Airport shuttle service when the rail link to this expanding airport opens in May 1991. The stock will be owned by BAA and will carry a new livery of white, with horizontal stripes in muted tones of green and grey, emblazoned with both the BAA and NSE logo's. Although mechanically and electrically identical to the 321s, they feature a revised interior layout with 2+2 (rather than 3+2) standard class seating, and large luggage areas.

Before commencement of the Stansted Express service, class 322 No. 322481 departs from Cambridge with a West Anglia service in October 1990. Chris Wilson

Class 411 '4 Cep' EMUs 1501 and 1549 depart from Dover Priory on 30th June 1990, forming the 14.06 Ramsgate—Charing Cross service. Thoroughly refurbished in the early 1980s, the aluminium window surrounds and tinted windows installed then enhance the NSE livery in which the leading unit is painted. The rear unit remains in the obsolete London and South East 'jaffa cake' colours. Alex Dasi-Sutton

Class 411 ('4 Cep') and 412 ('4 Bep')

Fleet Size: 120 × 4-car units (411), 7 × 4 car units (412).
Number Series: Class 411: 1500-1615, Class 412: 2301-2307.
Formation: Motor Standard + Trailer Standard + Trailer Brake Composite + Motor Standard.
In class 412 the Trailer Standard is replaced by a Trailer Buffet Standard.
Traction Equipment: 4 × English Electric 507
Maximum Speed: 90mph
Present Sphere of Operation: Class 411 Kent Coast, Class 412 Solent and Wessex.

This was the first large fleet of SR express EMUs utilising the Mark 1 bodyshell, and was constructed between 1956 and 1961 for the Modernisation Plan electrification of lines to the Kent Coast. Design-wise, they were extremely conservative, the layout being based firmly on that of the pre-War '4 Cor' units. They have standard SR EP brakes, EE507 traction motors on motor bogies mounted under the cab ends, and resistance control.

Following the experimental refitting of 7153 (now 1500) in 1975, all were thoroughly rebuilt at Swindon Works between 1980 and 1983. Entirely new interiors were fitted, and the guard's brake was moved from behind the driving cab to the composite trailer.

Solent and Wessex class 412 buffet EMU 2303 and class 421/5 'Greyhound' units. No.2303 is the only one of its type with Phase 2 style motor coaches incorporating tapered windscreens and shallow headcode panel. David Brown

Most of the 'Cep' fleet was painted in the two-tone brown 'jaffa cake' paint scheme between 1986 and 1988, and a number were fitted with new blue/orange stripe seat covers for the inauguration of the Hastings electrification in May 1986. Painting in NSE colours began only in 1988; these units, with their clean aluminium window frames and tinted glass, look particularly well in this livery. It is very sad therefore, that they have been particularly prone to graffiti-vandalism recently: happily, steps are now being taken to eradicate this.

Only seven class 412 ('4 Bep') buffet car units remained from the original 22 after rebuilding; the rest became class 411. Following rebuilding, class 412 was reallocated to the Waterloo-Portsmouth line. For the 'Portsmouth Express' timetable accelerations of 1989, most were rebogied with Mark 6 motor bogies and B5(S) trailer bogies to give an improved ride.

The buffet car from class 412 '4 Bep' 2307 is seen at Petersfield in the formation of the 09.06 Portsmouth Harbour—Waterloo train on 23rd September 1989. This view shows the corridor side, with a three-bay saloon followed by the buffet counter and a rather spartan 'lounge' area. When this photograph was taken, the vehicle had recently been re-equipped with new coil-sprung bogies to improve the riding qualities. David Brown

Class 413 ('4 Cap') and 414 ('2 Hap')

Fleet Size: 22 × 4 car-units (413), 23 ×2 car-units (414)
Number Series: 413: 3201-3213, 3301-3311. 414: 4201, 4301-4322.
Formation: 413: Driving Trailer Composite + Motor Brake Standard +
Motor Brake Standard + Driving Trailer Composite.
414: Motor Brake Standard + Driving Trailer Composite
Traction Equipment: 2 × English Electric 507 on outer bogie of each Motor Coach
Maximum Speed: 90mph
Present Sphere of Operation: 413 Kent Link and Kent Coast; 414 South Western Lines
(main line).

Nearly 200 '2 Hap' EMUs were constructed between 1957 and 1962, mainly for the Kent Coast electrification schemes. They have Mark 1 suburban-type bodyshells and 2+3 standard class seating, and although non-gangwayed have toilets in the driving trailer, one for each class. Standard SR traction equipment is fitted as are EP brakes. Many have now been withdrawn (the most recent ones being scrapped first, ironically), those remaining in unmodified form being used on South Western Lines main-line stopping services. While definitely anachronistic in 1990 for services such as Waterloo-Southampton, on which they are still used, the present stock shortage means that they will remain in service for some years yet, and they are currently undergoing heavy overhaul.

The 'Cap' units were formed in 1979 from pairs of 'Hap' units, with luggage vans innermost, initially for use on the 'Coastway' routes from Brighton. Originally keeping their first class accommodation at both ends, that at one end was declassified when they were transferred 'en masse' to the South Eastern in 1984. The units are now used largely on Charing Cross-Gillingham suburban services, which are standard class only! Although a few were withdrawn in 1990, like the 'Hap' stock, these units will be around for some time yet; probably being displaced by new class 471 express 'Networkers'.

Class 415 ('4 EPB') and 416 ('2 EPB')

Fleet Size: Class 415: Approx 200 4-car units, gradually reducing.
Class 416: Approx. 130 2-car units.
Number Series: 415, 51xx, 52xx, 54xx, 55xx, 56xx. 416: 62xx, 63xx, 64xx.
Formation: (Class 415) Motor Brake Standard + Trailer Standard +
Trailer Standard + Motor Brake Standard. (class 416) Motor Brake Standard +
Driving Trailer Standard (see text).
Traction Equipment: 4 × (class 415) or 2 × (class 416) EE507
Maximum Speed: 75mph (class 415/7 90mph)
Present Sphere of Operation: South London Lines; Oxted Line; Kent Link.

The first '4 EPB' was released from Eastleigh Works in 1950, and was the first SR EMU to have the EPB braking system and automatic buckeye couplers, the system which was standard up to the 1988 'Wessex Electrics'. Revolutionary in its electrics and pneumatics it might have been, but otherwise it was almost identical to what had gone before (the '4 Sub') and one wonders if passengers really noticed a difference apart from the slightly less jerky braking. Three of the Bulleid-bodied coaches were saloons, with 3+2 seating and centre gangway, while the other was a '6-a-side' compartment trailer. Over two hundred of this type (now class 415/1) were built up to 1957, many incorporating underframes and bogies salvaged from pre-War stock. Thirty-four 2-car units ('2 EPB', now all facelifted as class 416/3) were also built in 1959; these had all-saloon accommodation.

From 1954, ten-car trains were introduced on what are now Kent Link lines, and for this 100 '2 EPB's with BR mark 1 suburban bodyshells (now class 416/1) were built. Some 4-car units to this design were also constructed, but most have been withdrawn.

From 1981, a large proportion of the 'EPB' fleet has been 'facelifted', a low-cost refurbishment basically to improve the passenger environment. All compartments are converted to saloons, fluorescent strip-lighting and public-address are installed, the seats are re-upholstered with brighter moquette and new flooring is fitted. Of the different types, the entire fleet of class 416/3 and all remaining BR-design '4 EPBs' (classes 415/6 and 415/7) are so dealt with, as are nearly 100 Bulleid-design '4 EPBs' (class 415/4) and nine BR '2 EPBs' (class 416/4). The six units of class 415/7 differ from their sisters in being fitted with express gear ratio, allowing speeds of 90mph. A large reformation programme was undertaken for unrefurbished class 415/1 EMUs in 1988, following the murder of a young woman in a closed compartment; all compartment vehicles are now in separate class 415/5 units which are only used in the peaks, while class 415/1 are now all-saloon. The compartment vehicles have a red warning strip along the cantrail, and this has also spread to '2 EPB' units.

Unrefurbished units have reduced in number over the past few years, and the remainder do not have a long life, those with compartments hopefully going first. The fleet will be replaced in Kent Link services by new class 465 'Networker' units from 1991. Refurbished units, particularly those on South London Line services, are likely to last somewhat longer, and are now gradually being repainted in NSE livery, which does not sit well on these vehicles. SR-type '2 EPB' units work with class 423 'Vep' stock on East Grinstead line services, being fitted with window bars over the door droplights.

Class 421 ('4 Cig') and 422 ('4 Big')

Fleet Size: 133 × 4 car units (421), 18 × 4 car units (422)
Number Series: 11xx, 12xx, 13xx, 17xx, 18xx.
Formation: Driving Trailer Composite + Motor Standard + Trailer Standard + Driving Trailer Composite. In class 422, the Trailer Standard is replaced by a Trailer Buffet Standard.
Traction Equipment: 4 × English Electric 507
Maximum Speed: 90mph
Present Sphere of Operation: Sussex Coast; South Western Lines; Portsmouth Express (class 421 only).

The first 36 '4 Cig' and 12 '4 Big' units went into service on the Brighton line in 1965-66, replacing life-expired pre-War electric stock. Based on the mark 1 bodyshell, they differed from the 'Cep' units mainly in having a single motor coach at the centre of each unit, and a more modern cab with rounded edges and recessed jumper cables, moulded in reinforced fibreglass. They also rode on the latest coil-sprung B5S trailer bogies giving a much improved ride (EMU stock is notorious for rough riding). They were the last SR units to be delivered in green.

Further units of both types were built in 1971-74, again to replace old stock, this time on the Portsmouth 'direct' route and other South Western main-line services. Although basically similar to the earlier units, they had somewhat more spartan interiors. Between 1983 and 1984 the 'Bigs' were all transferred to Brighton line services and some of the later 'Cigs' work there also.

Following successful rebuilding of the 'Cep' units it was decided to refurbish some of the 'Cigs', but on a rather smaller scale. Improvements were restricted to new interior panelling and fluorescent strip lighting. The earlier units were done first, the first 11 being outshopped in L&SE 'jaffa cake' brown livery; 32 earlier units have so far been renovated, including some 'Bigs' which have been rebuilt as 'Cig' units, and 28 of the later series have also been done. Those numbered from 1301-1316 have been given minor electrical modifications to give them a (slightly) better performance for use on the accelerated 'Portsmouth Express' services which started in May 1989; they may be recognised externally by some rather unsightly black trim on the cab fronts.

Class 413 '4 Cap' EMUs 3204 and 3207 pass Factory Junction on a peak-hour Victoria to Dover Western Docks service in June 1989. Brian Morrison

Class 414 '2 Hap' EMUs 4321 and 4317 depart from Cosham with a special 11.07 Eastleigh— Portsmouth Harbour service on 6th May 1990, when a special Gala Day was held to commemorate the completion of the Solent Link electrification scheme. These useful units are generally used to make up 6- or 10-car trains formed otherwise of 'Vep' and 'Cig' stock on Solent and Wessex services. On SR 2- and 3-car multiple units, the inverted black triangle denotes the end with the luggage van.

'Facelifted' class 415/4 suburban unit 5452 leads the 14.47 Sidcup line service from Dartford into London Bridge on 13th May 1990. Built to the design of O.V.S. Bulleid in the early 1950s, the painting of these obsolete and unloved units into NSE livery began only in 1989 — the majority remain in blue and grey. Alex Dasi-Sutton

One of the class 421 '4 Cig' EMUs modified with better acceleration for Solent and Wessex express services, 1305 leads a Waterloo—Portsmouth service out of Cosham in May 1990. This subclass may be recognised by some extra black trim on the cab ends. Chris Wilson

Class 423 ('4 Vep')

Fleet Size: 195 × 4 car units
Number Series: 3401-3596, renumbered when rebuilt from 3001-3196.
Formation: Driving Trailer Composite + Motor Brake Standard +
Trailer Standard + Driving Trailer Standard.
Traction Equipment: 4 × English Electric 507
Maximum Speed: 90mph
Present Sphere of Operation: Kent Coast; Sussex Coast; Oxted line; Solent and Wessex.

The ubiquitous class 423 '4 Vep' units are the largest class of SR EMUs, and as the list above shows, can be seen on most parts of the third rail network. Based on the Mark 1 design and basically similar in layout to class 421, they have 3+2 seating in standard class with doors to each seating bay, and first class in compartments (although some of these have been downgraded in many units). The first 20 were built for stopping services on the newly-electrified Bournemouth line, entering service in 1967, and the very much larger batches were built, like the 'Cigs', to replace 1930s-built stock on the Brighton and Portsmouth lines. The final delivery was for lines in Kent, production finally finishing in 1974. As built, the 'Veps' had sliding ventilators on the large windows between the doors, but these became a maintenance liability and were sealed up. A few had these windows replaced by plain glass, giving the units concerned a somewhat different appearance.

A programme to refurbish the 'Vep' fleet was commenced early in 1988 in the workshops at Eastleigh, and is currently over half-way to completion. The main modification concerns the motor coach. As built, this had a very large brake van, generally far too capacious for present-day needs, and part of this is being converted into a two-bay standard class saloon, seating 18. An unusual feature is that there is only one door on each side of this saloon, and these doors are not opposite each other.

The SR operators like the 'Vep's, as they have a high-capacity to clear rush-hour crowds, and many doors to speed loading and unloading ('dwell time') at stations. Similar reasons make them unpopular with passengers, as the seating is cramped and the doors draughty. They are often worked indiscriminately with 'Cig' units, particularly on trains to the South Coast via Brighton. These useful EMUs are likely to remain in service until well into the next century.

Non-driving Motor Brake Standard 62218 from refurbished 'Vep' 3434, seen in Clapham Cutting on 25th November 1989. The new 18-seat standard class saloon in part of the former van area may be seen at the far end of the vehicle. David Brown

Class 431 ('6 Rep')

Fleet Size: 4 × 6-car units.
Number Series: 1903-1906.
Formation: Motor Standard + Trailer Brake Standard + Trailer First
+ Trailer Standard + Trailer Brake Standard + Driving Trailer Standard.
Traction Equipment: 4 × EE546 Traction Motors.
Maximum Speed: 90mph
Present Sphere of Operation: Solent and Wessex.

The story of this stock, originally introduced for the Bournemouth line electrification of 1967, is complicated. In order to provide through trains to Weymouth while avoiding the expense of electrification west from Branksome, a novel and ingenious traction arrangement was devised by the SR electrical and mechanical engineers. Fast trains were formed of a high-powered four-car motor unit with buffet car ('4 Rep') at the London end, hauling or pushing one or two unpowered 4-car trailer units ('4 TC') at the country end. In the down direction, the 'Rep' was detached at Bournemouth, and one or both of the TCs carried on over the non-electrified line to Weymouth, hauled by a push-pull fitted class 33/1 diesel-electric locomotive. In the reverse direction the locomotive pushed its train to Bournemouth where it was detached, the train continuing to Waterloo hauled by a 'Rep'. These arrangements came to an end in 1988 with the completion of the Bournemouth – Weymouth electrification, and the introduction of new class 442s to the route, these latter actually utilising traction motors recovered from '4 Rep' units. Only the motor coaches of the 'Reps' had been constructed new, the rest of the required vehicles have been rebuilt at Eastleigh or York from former Mark 1 locomotive-hauled stock. Some of the side-corridor firsts in the TCs were among the oldest such vehicles on BR. External styling was similar to the 'Cigs', with the same glass-fibre cab ends.

With not enough of the new class 442s to run the entire service, three '4 Rep' units were retained in traffic, one of which was involved in the Clapham accident in December 1988, one motor coach being written off. The other two 'Reps' were reformed and refurbished to incorporate the centre trailers from withdrawn class 438 units, and ran in this form until April 1990. For the Eastleigh – Portsmouth electrification of May 1990, four six car-units incorporating a 'Rep' motor coach at one end and various other 'Rep' and 'TC' trailer vehicles were formed.

Class 431 '6 Rep' units 1903 and 1906 draw through Clapham Junction in May 1990. Marshalled from 1967 Bournemouth line EMU vehicles to provide additional stock for the May 1990 'Solent Link' electrification, these EMUs are presently undergoing further reformation, the motor coach being moved from the front (seen here) to centre of the unit. David Brown

Class 442 ('5 Wes')

Fleet Size: 24 × 5 car units.
Number Series: 2401-2424.
Formation: Driving Trailer First + Trailer Standard + Motor Brake Buffet Standard + Trailer Standard + Driving Trailer Standard
Traction Equipment: 4 × English Electric 546
Maximum Speed: 100mph
Present Sphere of Operation: Wessex Electrics.

Class 442 '5 Wes' EMUs 2405 and 2421 pull away from Eastleigh. These were the first SR electric units with an official 100mph maximum speed, and the first on NSE to carry the new lighter shade of grey — even on the roofs. Note the lack of covers over the jumper-cable recesses on the unit ends, somewhat spoiling the streamlined appearance; it is hoped that these will be refitted eventually. David Brown

Interior of a standard class saloon in a class 442, showing 2+2 seating with 'blue blaze 1' moquette, arranged variously in face-to-face and unidirectional configurations. Note also the concealed lighting in the ceiling. NSE

These are the only EMUs on BR to be based on the standard BR Mark 3 23-metre-long bodyshell, and currently the only ones with full air-conditioning. They were built in 1988 for Waterloo-Bournemouth-Weymouth services, coinciding with electrification between Branksome and Weymouth. Although of very modern appearance, their equipment is entirely traditional, with EE546 traction motors recovered from withdrawn '4 Reps' (see above), camshaft-operated resistance control and electro-pneumatic brakes. They have standard SR brake and control jumpers mounted in recesses on the sleek cab fronts: originally covered over, the covers were temporarily removed early in 1989. The cab fronts are fitted with wrap-around windscreens and a through gangway connection, on top of which is a rather too small dot-matrix destination and headcode display which quickly became disused. The vehicles ride on bogies with air-bag suspension and give a far better ride than previous stock on the route, at speeds of up to 100mph.

Internally, they are the only Mark 3 vehicles with first class accommodation in compartments, and all vehicles feature full air-conditioning utilising a heat-pump system. The centre motor coach has a buffet with microwave for hot snacks, a small but pleasant 'lounge' area, a luggage van and guards' compartment, and a small standard class saloon. Elsewhere in the units are a disabled persons' toilet and a telephone. The class 442 'Wessex Electrics' are likely to remain the only examples of their breed, as future express stock will be based on the 'Networker' design.

Class 455

Fleet Size: 137 × 4 car units
Number Series: 455/8: 5801-5874, 455/7: 5701-5743, 455/9: 5901-5920.
Formation: Driving Trailer Standard + Motor Standard + Trailer Standard + Driving Trailer Standard.
Traction Equipment: 4 × English Electric traction motors under Motor Coach.
Maximum Speed: 75mph
Present Sphere of Operation: South London Lines (455/8 only); South Western Lines inner and some outer-suburban.

Class 455 was the new 'standard' SR suburban EMU using the Mark 3 sliding door bodyshell. They are fitted with standard EE 507 traction motors, many of them recovered from old stock and reconditioned, and have separate waist-level control and brake hoses, rather than fully integral couplers. Most have standard camshaft resistance control, but 5916-20 were experimentally fitted with thyristor 'chopper' control, and 5912 was the electrical testbed for the class 319 'Thameslink' units. Internally, they have low-backed suburban seating but no toilets.

The first of these units (455/8) were introduced from 1983 onwards to replace older 'Sub' and 'EPB' stock, initially on South Western (SW) suburban services out of Waterloo. From May 1985 the first 36 were gradually transferred to the Central services out of Victoria and London Bridge. Class 455/7 were delivered in 1984, and included a trailer from a Class 508 unit, and class 455/9 in 1985. Both these latter types work purely on South Western Lines services.

The early units were widely criticised for poor standards of design and construction, the front end (basically the same as class 317/1) being particularly hideous. This latter feature was improved greatly on classes 455/7 and 455/9. The last batch also had various other detail changes, including improved doors and full length guttering, a seemingly minor feature which improved their appearance no end. The NSE colour scheme has also made these units appear much more attractive.

Since late 1987, unit 5824 has been fitted experimentally with various proposed 'Networker' fittings. One vehicle has high-backed seats arranged in various configurations and new flooring. Very readable cab-end dot matrix destination and headcode displays are fitted, as well as internal electronic information displays.

Class 455/8 unit 5821, one of the original batch of this class, seen at the historic 'listed' station at Crystal Palace in May 1989. R.C. Riley

The final batch of 20 class 455 units for the SR were built without internal pressure-ventilation fans, and therefore have prominent air inlets along the roofs. The last few of the class to be painted in NSE colours were given an improved livery with an extra white stripe above the cantrail red stripe (similar to class 319). This feature can clearly be seen on 5901, arriving at Guildford off the 'new' line via Cobham with the 14.42 from Waterloo on 19th May 1990. David Brown

Class 456

Fleet Size: 24 × 2-car units.
Number Series: 456001-456024
Formation: Motor Standard – Driving Trailer Standard.
Traction Equipment: 2 × GEC (EE) 507
Maximum Speed: 75mph
Sphere of Operation: South London Lines.

This small class is likely to be the final flowering of the Mark 3-derived EMU design, and is due off the York production line in 1991 after completion of the 4-car 319/321 contracts.

Although having the 321-type bodyshell with non-gangwayed cab ends and plug-type driver's doors, they will be fitted with waist-level external jumper cables to permit coupling with the SR class 455 fleet. As may be seen from the artist's impression, a reasonable job has been made of incorporating these onto the front end design. Showing how far the NSE standards for suburban stock have progressed, class 456 will feature high-backed seating and a toilet, neither of which the 455s (designed before the advent of NSE) possess! Electrically, the new units will have GEC Gate-Turn-Off Thyristor control equipment and yet another version of the type 507 traction motor.

An artist's impression of the new class 456 two-car units for South London Lines services, delivery of which was about to commence as we went to press. The basic non-gangwayed '321' style front end has been utilised, but with the necessary (but ugly) jumper cables for multiple working with 455s superimposed onto it. NSE

Class 483

Fleet Size: 10 × 2-car units
Number Series: 483 001-010
Formation: Motor Standard + Motor Standard.
Present Sphere of Operation: Island Line.

The remaining stub of BR-owned railway on the Isle of Wight, between Ryde Pier Head and Shanklin, was electrified as from March 1967. Train services were operated by a fleet of ex-LT 'Standard Stock' tube cars, generally dating from the 1920s, formed into 7-car units. Standard-sized rolling stock could not be utilised due to limited clearances in Ryde Tunnel, made worse when the track was raised to prevent flooding. Originally given a life expectancy of 10 years, the fleet was gradually reduced in size but the last of these vintage vehicles was not finally withdrawn until 1990, and one remains in use as a 'Sandite' train.

It was inevitable that further redundant LT tube stock would be refurbished for use on the Island, and following much rumour and counter-rumour, vehicles of 1938 'EHO' tube stock were purchased by BR in October 1988. The stock was in somewhat worse condition than BR had hoped, and the first new two-car unit, now classified 483, did not emerge until July 1989 after a thorough refurbishment at BRML Eastleigh.

Most of the refurbishment work took place internally, where new panelling and strip-lighting was installed. Passenger door control buttons were also reinstated. Externally, the 'new' trains look very smart in NSE stripes. Ride is obviously much improved over the old stock, as is acceleration.

Opposite **Refurbished interior of car 221 of unit 483001 at Shanklin. The interior panelling and flooring have been completely renewed, the seats reupholstered in 'blue blaze 1' moquette, and fluorescent strip lighting and passenger door buttons installed.** David Brown

Class 487

Number Series: 51-62 (motors), 71-86 (trailers)
Trains do not run in fixed formations, but normally a Motor Brake Standard is formed each end of three Trailer Standards.
Traction Equipment: EE500
Present Sphere of Operation: Waterloo and City Line.

The Waterloo and City Line is a deep level 'tube' railway running 1½ miles from Waterloo to Bank. Opened in 1900 as a separate undertaking, it was quickly absorbed by the LSWR, and via the SR eventually passed into British Railways' (and hence NSE) hands. It is the only London tube line not operated by LRT, although it appears on the Underground system map. Presently, the line operates Mondays to Fridays and Saturday mornings.

The class 487 stock presently in service dates from 1940, when it replaced vehicles built for the opening. Of Bulleid design, the motor coaches have cabs at both ends, although they no longer work singly in the off-peak. Internally, there are plenty of grab-rails and a limited number of rather spartan seats, with characteristic scalloped tops. Although they have been re-bogied once in their lives, the ride remains poor (and noisy!). Originally clad in green rexine (a leathercloth material) with aluminium ends and trim, they went through the green and blue eras. A minor refurbishment scheme was carried out in 1987, and the '487's now carry NSE stripes. This work was partly paid for by Allied-Lyons, whose logo appeared prominently on the car exteriors for a time.

Opposite **Obviously a problem to replace due to the small size and specialised nature of the fleet, these 50-year-old EMUs are to be superseded by a small batch of vehicles built to the same design as London Underground's new Central Line replacement stock by BREL.** Brian Morrison

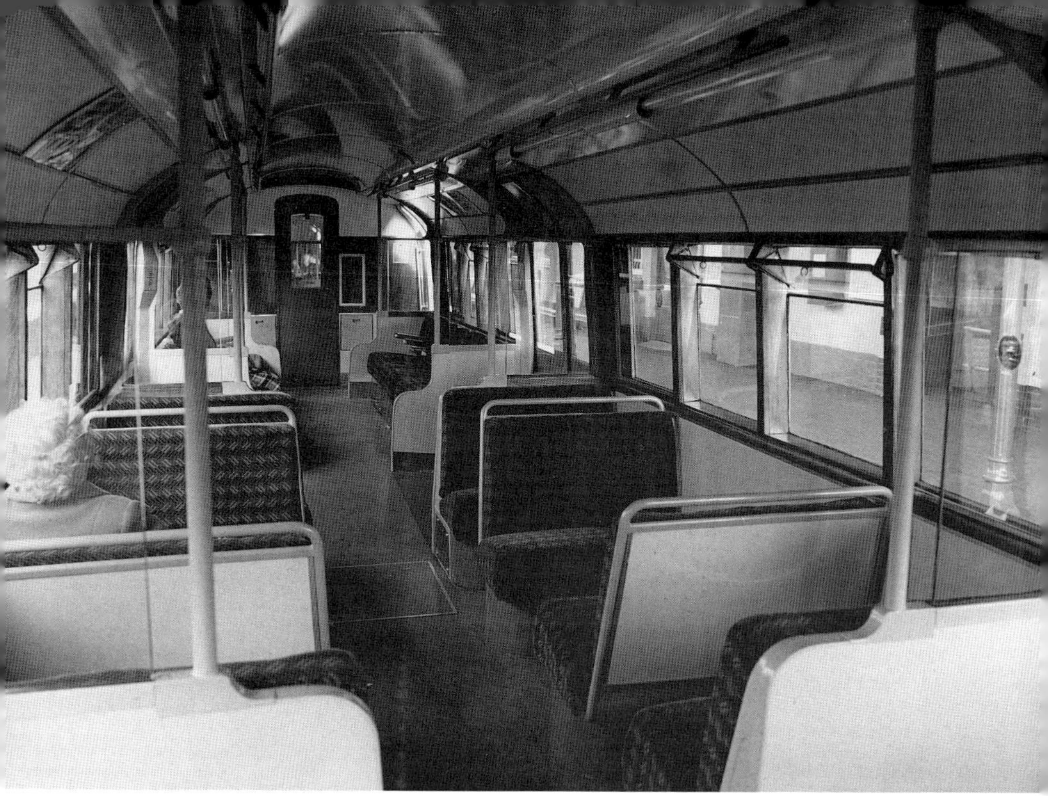

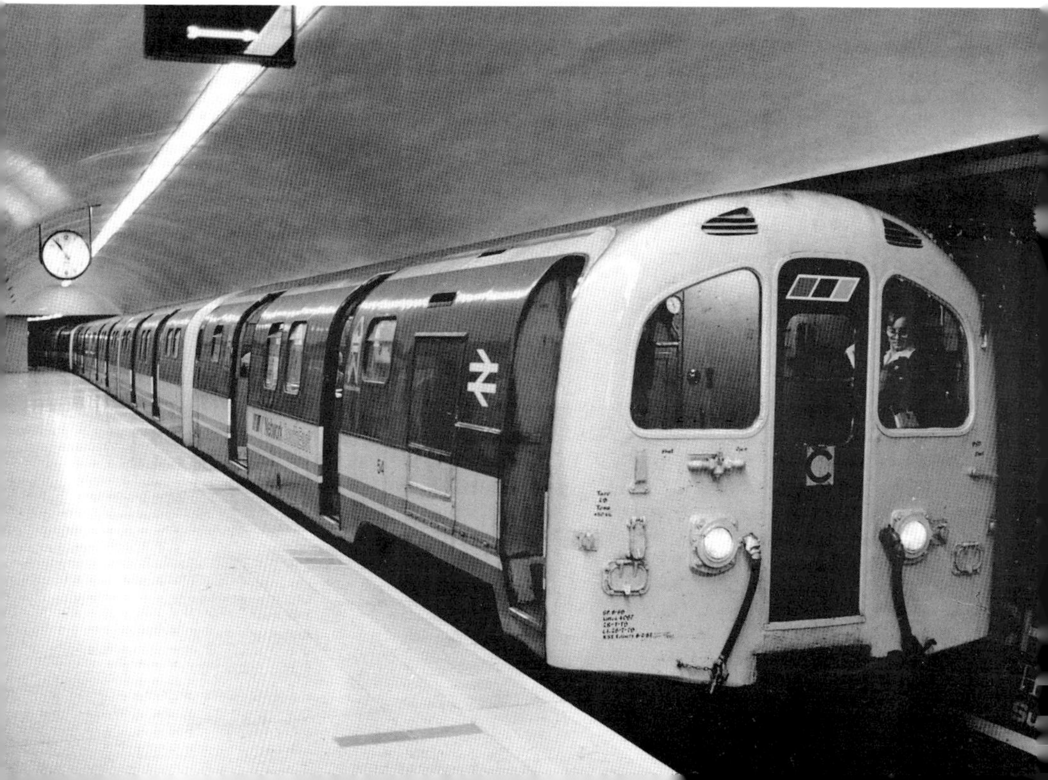
54
C

DIESEL MULTIPLE UNITS

Diesel multiple units on NSE are of two major types with totally different transmission systems. Those built for Southern Region routes (classes 205 and 207) are diesel-electric, having a large 600hp diesel engine mounted in the body supplying electric traction motors in a motor bogie via a generator. There is much commonality of parts with contemporary SR EMUs, and the vehicles are based on the suburban Mark 1 bodyshell, with side-doors to each seating bay, and an interior similar to a '4 EPB' EMU.

Those diesel units built for other Regions (classes 101-122) generally have mechanical transmission, with small diesel engines mounted underfloor driving the wheels through a gearbox. They thus sound (and smell) much like buses. Body designs vary, but are generally of fairly lightweight construction. Unlike the SR units, they are often not in fixed formations, with vehicles being swapped freely between units. Although some classes (115, 117 etc) are indiginous to the London area, others have been drafted in from other areas of the country, when those parts obtained newer stock! Good examples of this are the class 104 units, which were utilised for many years between Manchester and Buxton – they may now be seen between Gospel Oak and Barking, or occasionally on 'Thames' services.

Although the number of DMU vehicles working on Network SouthEast services will gradually drop, they will be in use on non-electrified lines for the foreseeable future, and some of new design ('Network Turbo' Class 165) have been ordered. Express-type DMUs, classes 166 and 171, are also likely to take over services presently loco-hauled in the next few years.

Note that although the majority of DMMUs working in the NSE area carry unit numbers on the front ends, vehicles can be and frequently are mixed up to keep trains in service, as all have compatible brakes and MU control systems.

Below **One of the three-car class 101 DMUs allocated to North Downs services, L832 approaches Guildford with a Reading-Gatwick service in May 1990.** David Brown

Facing Page **A very smart-looking Birmingham RCW-built class 104 twin unit L702 approaches Acton in August 1989, forming an afternoon Paddington to Slough service. A class 121 single unit has been added to the rear to make up a three-car set.** Hugh Dady

Class 101

Fleet Size: Approx. 62 vehicles, variously formed into 2-3-and-4 car sets.
Power: 2 × Leyland or AEC engines under each motor coach.
Maximum Speed: 75mph
Present Sphere of Operation: Thames; North Downs; North London Line (Gospel Oak-Barking); Great Eastern (Colchester St Botolphs-Sudbury); West Anglia (Cambridge-King's Lynn).

A design also found on many other parts of BR, the NSE vehicles of this class are part of a large fleet introduced between 1956 and 1959, although it has been only in the last decade that they have become common in the London area. They have 3+2 seating in standard class and 2+2 in first class, both in open saloons, but not having been originally designed for intensive suburban operations, generally have only two passenger doors on the side of each vehicle, opening into transverse vestibules (an arrangement known as 'low density' by BR, and also found on classes 104 and 108). They have shallower cab windscreens and a rounder body profile than other DMMU classes, and characteristic aluminium surrounds to the side windows.

The three-car units, formed Motor Brake Standard – Trailer Standard – Motor Composite, are based at Reading for use on Reading-Gatwick Airport/Tonbridge 'North Downs' trains, although they turn up on Paddington-area suburban workings also. The two-car units, formed Motor Brake Standard – Driving Trailer or Motor Composite, are generally used on 'Thames' workings, and on Gospel Oak-Barking and Colchester-Sudbury trains.

Class 104

Fleet Size: Approx. 10 vehicles, formed into 2-car sets, or as substitutes in sets of other classes.
Power: 2 × Leyland 150hp under each motor coach.
Present Sphere of Operation: North London Lines (Gospel Oak-Barking); Chiltern Lines, Thames Lines.

Built by Birmingham RC&W, these units, all of which are 2-car, can be recognised by having an upright front end. All are now standard class only, but the 3+2 seating in dingy saloons is particularly poor anyway. Like the 101s, they have only a few doors. Dating from 1957, they do not have a long future on NSE.

Class 108 'Derby Lightweight'
Fleet Size: Approx. 9 × 2-car sets.
Power: 2 × Leyland 150hp under each motor coach.
Maximum Speed: 75mph
Present Sphere of Operation: Chiltern Lines; Three Counties (Kettering-Bedford-Bletchley),

Another ubiquitous type found also found on other parts of the BR network, these units are similar in concept and layout to the Metro-Cammell class 101, but have the same front end as class 119 etc and deeper side windows. Built between 1958 and 1961 at Derby, they are of lightweight construction (hence the title), when compared to the otherwise similar class 107, none of which work on NSE. They are generally formed Motor Brake Second – Driving Trailer Composite, and some DTCs also work with class 115 motor coaches on Chiltern Lines. Based at Bletchley, their main work is on the rural Bedford-Bletchley service, with some trains extended to/from Kettering.

Class 115
Fleet Size: 23 × 4-car units.
Power: 2 × Leyland Albion 200hp under each motor coach.
Maximum Speed: 75mph
Present Sphere of Operation: Chiltern Lines.

These 1960 BR Derby-built DMMUs have always worked on the Chiltern Lines services from Marylebone to Aylesbury and High Wycombe/Banbury. Most are formed into 4-car units, formed of two Motor Brake Standards flanking a Standard Class Trailer and a Composite, only the latter having a toilet. There is a door to each seating bay with large plain glass windows between. There are generally no gangways between vehicles (although these have recently been fitted to a few) and the seating is of heavier construction with higher backs than in other classes (such as '117') which these units otherwise superficially resemble. A small number of Motor Coaches work with Driving Trailer Composites of class 108, which have fewer doors and 2+2 seating in first class. Based at Bletchley, they are likely to be withdrawn in 1991, being replaced by class 165.

Class 117
Fleet Size: 30 × 3 coach units.
Unit Numbers: L400-L429.
Traction Equipment: 2 × Leyland 150hp engines under each motor coach.
Maximum Speed: 75mph
Present Sphere of Operation: Thames Lines.

Formed Motor Brake Standard – Trailer Composite – Motor Standard, these units were introduced to Western Region suburban services out of Paddington in 1959-1960, and have remained on these workings ever since. They have suburban 3+2 high density seating in open saloons in standard class, and 2+1 in first class, both classes with side doors to each seating bay. A pair of toilets separates the classes in the centre car. They were fitted with gangways around 1970. All are now in NSE livery. The odd class 116 car also works in this fleet, but other than a different builder (BR Derby) they are all but identical. Although one of the tidier-looking classes of DMMU, they are due to be withdrawn in 1991-92, being replaced by class 165 'Network Turbo'.

On a typical duty for the type, a class 108 twin-unit with Driving Motor Brake Standard 51916 leading runs into Woburn Sands on 10th June 1989, forming a Bletchley—Bedford 'Three Counties' train. Alex Dasi-Sutton

The class 117 three-car suburban units have been on 'Thames' local services out of Paddington for 30 years, and are shortly to be replaced by class 165 'Network Turbos'. On a typical duty for the type, units L405 and L418 accelerate away from West Drayton, forming the 09.35 Reading—Paddington on 28th April 1990. David Brown

Class 119

Fleet Size: 8 × 3-car units.
Unit Numbers: In series L575-L596
Traction System: 2 × Leyland 150hp motors under each motor coach
Maximum Speed: 75mph
Present Sphere of Operation: North Downs.

Known as 'cross country' DMMUs by BR, these units have superior accommodation, featuring 2+2 seating with armrests in standard class. Formed Motor Brake Composite – Trailer Standard – Motor Standard, they were transferred to the Reading-Tonbridge/Gatwick Airport services in 1980, bringing diesel-mechanical units regularly to the SR on a daily basis. They are particularly useful for airport services because they have a vast van space – this has been added to by stripping out the former buffet counter in the centre trailer as a 'Railair Passenger Luggage' area.

Although numbers have fallen, and their work on the North Downs line is now shared with 3-car class 101 units, they are likely to be in service for a few more years. They will probably be displaced by electrification, as NSE plans currently show Reading-Redhill for completion in 1993.

Class 121

Fleet Size: 11 single motor coaches; 9 driving trailers optionally work with them.
Unit Numbers: L120-L131.
Traction System: 2 × 150hp Leyland engines.
Maximum Speed: 75mph
Present Sphere of Operation: Thames Lines.

To the same basic design as the class 117, and also built by Pressed Steel, these single motor cars have a driving cab at each end, a small van, and a standard class saloon. Designed for branch line use, they can be made up to two-cars with addition of a standard class driving trailer, and can also sometimes be seen sustituted into class 101 or 117 sets in place of their 'proper' motor coach. They are also due to be replaced by class 165 in 1991. Although all are now in Network stripes, some have the up-sweep at the vehicle ends, whereas others do not. Their usual work is on the Paddington-Greenford stopping services and on WR branches between Paddington and Reading.

Class 159 *Due 1992*

Until recently, Network SouthEast's rolling stock replacement strategy for the Waterloo – Salisbury – Exeter line was to supersede the class 50 locomotives and mark 2 coaches presently operating the service by specially developed class 171 'Network Turbo' (similar to class 166) diesel units sometime in the mid-1990s. Due to the increasing unreliability and maintenance costs of the '50' fleet, however, their replacement has become a matter of urgency.

It has therefore been decided to divert the last 66 vehicles of the class 158 'Express' DMU order, presently under construction for Regional Railways, to NSE. With 6 additional coaches, these will be made up into twenty-four 3-car units, reclassified 159 and carrying the brand-name 'Western Turbo', for the West of England line. They should all be in service by the end of 1992, and are likely to be maintained at a new depot at Salisbury. With a 90mph maximum speed, lightweight 23m long aluminum bodyshells, power-operated 'plug' doors and full air-conditioning, class 159 fits in well with the 'Networker' concept anyway, and the underfloor power and drive systems are similar to those of the class 165 units. Otherwise virtually identical to the 158s, the Network Units will have an improved first class section with 2 + 1 seating and tables, and a similar interior colour scheme to the class 442 'Wessex Electrics'.

Gloucester-built class 119 'cross country' DMMU L580 in Network livery. Although outdated, these units have particularly sumptuous seating, as well as large areas for passengers' luggage, important on the Reading—Gatwick service. Alex Dasi-Sutton

A single-car version of class 117 for light branch-line use, and like them built by Pressed Steel, the NSE examples of class 121 are used on 'Thames' local services. Here, L129 idles in the cavernous atmosphere of the suburban platforms at Paddington on 4th June 1990, waiting to depart with the 14.36 stopping service to Greenford.
David Brown

A full size mock up of a 165 'Network Turbo' car at the works of BREL, Derby. These diesel vehicles are being used to renew the stock on services from Paddington and Marylebone starting in 1991. BREL Ltd

Class 205 ('3H')

Fleet Size: 20 × 3-car units.
Numbers: In the range 205001-033, 205101.
Traction System: 600hp Diesel engine, driving two EE 507 traction motors.
Maximum Speed: 75mph
Present Sphere of Operation: Oxted Line; Solent and Wessex, Marsh Link, Clapham Junction-Kensington Olympia.

Originally two-car units but with most soon made up to three coaches due to traffic increases, the '3H' DEMUs were introduced from 1957, initially on non-electrified lines in the Hampshire area (hence their SR designation). Formed Driving Motor Brake Standard – Trailer Standard – Driving Trailer Composite, they are basically a diesel engined version of the class 414 '2 Hap' EMU, but have one half of the motor coach taken up by the engine compartment and guard's accommodation. Thus they have Mark 1 bodyshells with side-doors to each seating bay and identical 3+2 seating to older suburban EMUs. There are some variations in accommodation – the last units built (originally 1127-33, now 205 027-033) have a larger brake van and thus one less seating bay in the motor coach, while five units have only two first class compartments, the third being empty and used as a luggage area.

In 1980, unit 1111 was thoroughly rebuilt at Eastleigh Works, probably as a costing exercise. New interior panelling, fluorescent lighting and reprofiled seats were fitted, and the first class saloon. Gangways between vehicles were fitted. No more have been done, and this unique unit, now 205 101, is generally used on 'Marsh Link' services between Ashford and Hastings, where its through gangways facilitate ticket issuing and checking by conductor.

The 205s have had a wide usage over the years, at one time even regularly operating as far afield as Bristol. At the time of writing, the class is used on Oxted Line Oxted-Uckfield (including through workings to/from London in the peaks), Marsh Link, Reading-Basingstoke, Salisbury-Southampton and Clapham Junction-Kensington Olympia services. They occasionally appear also on Waterloo-Salisbury trains, where their seating and toilet accommodation are clearly inadequate!

Class 207 ('3D')

Fleet Size: 8 × 3-car units.
Number Series: 207 001-017
Traction System: English Electric 600hp Diesel engine driving two EE 507 traction motors.
Maximum Speed: 75mph
Present Sphere of Operation: Oxted Line; Solent and Wessex.

This fleet, originally of 19 units, was built to replace steam traction on non-electrified lines in East Sussex, centred around Oxted and Tunbridge Wells West. Although generally similar to class 205, they were built with slightly narrower bodies, permitting only 2+2 seating in standard class. This was to enable units to negotiate a narrow tunnel at Tunbridge Wells, on a route now closed. The accommodation is also arranged differently, with the first class compartments and toilet in the middle of the centre trailer. They also have a (slightly) more attractive front end, moulded in reinforced GRP, with rounded corners and recesses for the jumper cables.

With the electrification of the East Grinstead line in 1987, many of the class were withdrawn, and they are now split between Selhurst and Eastleigh Depots, working indiscriminately with the 205s. Those based at Eastleigh have had two first class compartments downgraded. Their future is also the same as their wider sisters, although as they have among the roughest-riding bogies in the fleet, they may well be withdrawn first.

Solent and Wessex Class 205 '3H' DEMU 205033 approaches Mortimer forming a Reading to Basingstoke service. A half-hourly stopping service on this line commenced with the May 1990 timetable using additional DEMUs made spare by the 'Solent Link' electrification. David Brown

Unit 207001 at Clapham Junction at rest between peak hour Kensington Olympia shuttle services in October 1990. Alex Dasi-Sutton

Resplendent in the latest version of NSE locomotive livery, class **47/4** diesel-electric **47 581** is seen near Millbrook with a Weymouth-Swansea train in July 1990. Alex Dasi-Sutton

All remaining NSE-allocated class **50** locomotives are now based at Plymouth Laira (way outside the NSE area) for working Waterloo—Salisbury—Exeter services. On 31st March 1990, No.**50 018** *Resolution* was photographed powering through Winchfield in charge of the 14.15 Waterloo—Salisbury, formed of mark **2** coaches. David Brown

Top **50 007** was named *Sir Edward Elgar* and painted in Great Western lined green livery in 1985 as part of the GW150 celebrations, and has had special dispensation from the Sector Director to remain in this livery. On 28th April 1990, this celebrity (but none too reliable) locomotive hauls the 16.15 Waterloo – Salisbury service away from Clapham Junction, unusually routed via the slow lines due to engineering work. David Brown

Above **No.73 134** *Woking Homes 1885-1985* in Clapham cutting in June 1990. Hugh Dady

Left **Among miscellaneous shunting locomotives allocated to NSE are the two remaining class 03 diesel shunters, both resident on the Isle of Wight for use on ballast trains etc.** David Brown

LOCOMOTIVES

As stated earlier, it is NSE policy to reduce the number of locomotive-hauled services it operates, and most if not all are likely to be replaced during the next decade, mainly by diesel-powered 'Networker' derivatives of classes 166 and 171. Thus the number of locomotives, which at present only consist of three main types (classes 47, 50 and 73), is expected to gradually diminish, especially as all three classes are reaching the ends of their useful lives.

As mentioned, the numbers of all three classes operated by NSE are members of larger fleets, and thus locomotives of the same classes belonging to other Sectors may be seen working on Network tracks. Examples of this include class 47 on InterCity inter-regional services through Oxford and Reading to Basingstoke, Southampton and Poole, and class 73 on InterCity 'Gatwick Express' services between Victoria and Gatwick Airport.

Class 47

Fleet Size: 18
Traction Equipment: Diesel-electric-Sulzer 2580hp diesel with Brush Traction Motors
Wheel Arrangement: CoCo
Present Sphere of Operation: Thames Lines (Paddington-Oxford/Newbury).

The Network SouthEast examples of this class form but a small fraction of the most numerous type of main line Diesel-electric locomotive on BR today. Built by Brush at Loughborough and by BREL at Crewe between 1962 and 1967, they are the standard high powered mixed-traffic workhorse on BR.

NSE-allocated examples are mainly of one type, subclass 47/4. These are fitted with electric train heating, and may be seen on trains from Paddington to Oxford (Birmingham) and Newbury (NWRA pool, based at Old Oak Common).

A fleet of sixteen classs 47/7s were converted from standard locomotives to work push-pull services on the Scottish Region Edinburgh-Glasgow route (and later others). They are fitted with an early version of the 'Time Division Multiplexing' (TDM) system of MU control, whereby signals to control the loco from a remote cab are fed along the train lighting cables, a versatile system as hauled vehicles being used do not need to be specially adapted. With the planned introduction of class 158 'Express' DMUs to the ScotRail routes, the class 47/7s are being transferred south to NSE duties out of Paddington, although the TDM equipment is sadly not being utilised. After overhaul and repaint, the 47 705 and 47 714 re-entered service in 1989 – the rest following in 1990. The class can be recognised by the pair of lighting jumpers on the cab fronts.

Most of the NSE fleet of class 47s is now in the owning sector's colours – in particular, large numbers of NWRA locos were repainted into the latest dark blue scheme without curved upsweeps during 1989 and 1990.

Class 50

Fleet Size: 22 locomotives
Traction Equipment: Diesel-electric – English Electric 2700hp engine driving English Electric traction motors.
Wheel Arrangement: CoCo.
Maximum Speed: 100mph
Present Sphere of Operation: West of England; Thames (London-Oxford/Newbury).

These 2700hp locomotives were built by English Electric in 1967-68, being based on their successful 'DP2' prototype, and were originally leased to BR by their builders. Initially used in the North West, particularly on West Coast Anglo-Scottish services between Crewe and Glasgow prior to electrification north of Weaver Junction in

1974, they were then transferred down to the Western Region, where they took over from Diesel-hydraulic classes, and were given 'Warship' names. Never particularly reliable, due to the insistence by BR on the fitting of much complex equipment which the prototype did not have, they were put through a thorough refurbishment programme at Doncaster between 1979 and 1983. The most obvious external alterations to the refurbished examples were the central high-intensity headlamp on the cab fronts, and from 50 023 'Howe' onwards, the adoption of what became known as the 'large logo' blue livery, an attractive colour scheme which suited these locomotives well.

With the introduction of class 253 High Speed Trains from Paddington to the West Country, class 50s began to be used on the Waterloo-Salisbury-Exeter two-hourly expresses from 1980, where they replaced the smaller SR class 33s, and this route is now their main 'fief'. From May 1989 they again displaced class 33s on the Waterloo-Salisbury semi-fasts, so virtually all trains west of Basingstoke on this route are worked by these good-looking and capable locomotives. All are now allocated to the NSSA (Solent and Sarum) pool for working these services, their use on Paddington-Oxford/Newbury 'Networker Express' having ended in mid-1990.

50 023 was painted in an early version of Network stripes for the launch of NSE on 10th June 1986, and locomotives are in one of three variations of NSE livery. An exception is 50 007, which has been given special dispensation by the Network Director to remain in the non-standard GW green in which it was painted in 1984, when it was also renamed 'Sir Edward Elgar'. It is proposed that 50 050 will be restored to near original external condition, with original blue livery, for its final months in service

Class 73

Fleet Size: 8 locomotives
Traction Equipment: 4 × 400hp EE546 traction motors, working off 750V dc third-rail supply. Auxiliary 600hp diesel generator.
Wheel Arrangement: BoBo.
Maximum Speed: 80mph
Present Sphere of Operation: Solent and Wessex.

An interesting design of hybrid locomotive designed specifically to suit Southern Region operating conditions, the first of six members of what is now class 73/0 was delivered in 1962. The main production batch, which differed in some details from the prototypes and is now classified 73/1 or 73/2 depending on usage, was introduced as part of the Bournemouth line electrification in 1967, and built by English Electric at Newton-le-Willows. Basically straight 1420hp electric locomotives running of the SR 660/750V dc third-rail supply, they are fitted with a 600hp diesel generator for running at reduced power 'off the juice', There is considerable commonality of parts with contemporary EMUs. For instance, they have Mark 6 power bogies, are fitted with the same EE546 traction motors as the 'Reps' and 442s and have EP brakes with waist-level jumpers. Thus they can work in multiple with the majority of SR EMU stock.

Although all allocated to SR depots, most of the fleet are allocated to regional departmental or InterCity (class 73/2) pools, the latter for working the 'Gatwick Express' and other miscellaneous duties, such as hauling the 'Venice Simplon Orient Express' Pullman train. Apart from miscellaneous duties, NSE's locomotives can be seen hauling the Ocean Liner boat train between Waterloo and Southampton Docks. Although, with their dual-power capability, the class 73s are a versatile type, with the exception of the InterCity 73/2 subclass, they seem to be 'nobody's babies' these days, and they are not expected to last long.

Most of the class carry the 'Main Line' version of InterCity livery, but only a few carry the latest variation. There are a large number of non-standard liveries.

HAULED COACHING STOCK

As with locomotives, the quantity of hauled coaching stock owned by Network SouthEast will gradually diminish as electrification schemes are completed and more multiple units are introduced. Of the four basic types in service on BR, NSE utilised the earlier types Mark 1 and Mark 2. Basic descriptions of these appear in the 'Electric Multiple Units' section of this chapter, but to briefly recap:-

Mark 1: Separate underframe, generally 64ft long. Body of welded steel construction, gradual curve to body profile. Bogies are of various types, the most numerous being 'Commonwealth', which have heavy cast steel frames and coil springs; and 'B4' which also have coil springing, but frames fabricated from strip.

Mark 2: Integral body with separate underframe, again 64ft in length. Straight sides with pronounced curve inwards at bottom, and domed ends to roof. All ride on 'B4' bogies. There are various sub-types to this design: Mark 2/2A have narrow doors, Mark 2B/2C have wider doors which wrap around the coach corners.

Internally, 'open' vehicles have 2+2 seating either side of a central gangway, those in Mark 2 being of a distinctive (and comfortable) design with winged headrests – these are not found in any equivalent EMU stock. Some Mark 2 standard class vehicles have seats recovered from the abortive APT. 'Corridor' coaches have a side corridor and compartments – Mark 1 standard class compartments of this type seat either three (with folding armrests) or four each side. First class compartments seat three each side. Those on the Waterloo-Salisbury-Exeter line (NSSX) have been refurbished, with removable seat covers and murals by Edward Pond (as in various EMU classes).

In addition, there are two General Utility Van (GUV) allocated to NSE – these have slab sides, no gangways and are used to convey luggage on the Ocean Liner boat trains etc.

Proudly displaying a 'West of England' line badge, integral-bodied Mark 2A Corridor Brake First (BFK) 17074 stands at Waterloo in December 1989 on an Exeter service. This is typical of the vehicles used on this route, and has refurbished compartments with Edward Pond murals. Chris Wilson

NETWORKER: THE HUMAN TRAIN

At the launch of Network SouthEast in June 1986 the Sector Director, Chris Green, promised customers a new concept for suburban rail travel around London. Dubbed 'Networker' these new trains, which would appear in several versions, would be designed 'from the ground up' with the customer in mind – that is, to a commercial specification first and foremost. Most of the rolling stock inherited by NSE had been designed by engineers for engineers, with the passenger coming second.

The NSE design team took until December 1987 to show the public what it had in mind, when a mock-up of the proposed class 465, to be used on Southern Region suburban lines in Kent, was unveiled at Victoria station. The external design was certainly a world apart from what went before, with a modernistic but attractive front end and plug doors which closed flush into the bodywork. Internally, the seats were generally laid out in the 3+2 configuration either side of a central gangway, but with some longitudinal and 2+2 near the door vestibules to give a wider gangway near the exits, and were to a new design with one-piece high backs. The seats also actually line up with the windows! A new non-slip flooring was used and there were plenty of hanging grips and rails for standing passengers. Internal dot-matrix information and destination displays were fitted, although development of these has caused problems, and the first three tranches at least of these units are not likely to have them. Similar technology was used for a large display (including headcode) on the front of the train. Each unit (it was originally intended that there would be 2- 3- and 4-car versions to give flexibility in train formation) will be gangwayed between vehicles, but not at cab ends.

Technically, the class 465 is to incorporate features which will give a higher first cost, but lower running costs due to energy saving and decreased maintenance. Bodywork is to be of welded lightweight aluminium alloy construction to save weight over conventional steel construction. Power will be by micro-processor controlled three-phase AC traction motors, with half the axles (rather than the present norm of 25% with dc drive) powered. This will be possible because AC motors are both lighter and simpler to maintain. A side benefit will be increased adhesion, hopefully doing away completely with problems of autumn leaf-fall. Couplings will be completely automatic, including brake and MU control connections, and the trains will be designed for driver-only operation (DOO).

Various Networker systems have been tried out in experimental vehicles. As already mentioned, one trailer of 455 5824 is fitted out with Networker-style seating and flooring, and this unit also has internal and external dot-matrix displays, the former not particularly reliable as yet, but that is the purpose of prototypes! Two test-beds for rival Brush and GEC three-phase drive were converted from existing stock in 1988, and ran on trial on the SR during 1989, including a spell in passenger service on the Waterloo-Windsor line. Both units were lettered 'Traction Development for the 1990s'. Unit 457 001 was formed from redundant class 210 DEMU (generally similar to class 317/1) vehicles and a trailer from 455 5920, and has Brush equipment mounted under the driving cars. The rest of 5920 formed the GEC test unit, with an ex-210 centre vehicle with the new motors. Late in 1989, the former unit had a 313-type pantograph-fitted trailer vehicle marshalled into it, and as 316 999 commenced tests under 25kV AC catenary between Colchester and Clacton.

The first firm orders for 'Network' type vehicles were actually for diesel-powered versions, dubbed 'Network Turbo'. Seventy-seven vehicles of class 165 have been ordered for Chiltern Line Services out of Marylebone, as one part of a total renewal for the line (also including track signalling etc), and the first should enter service in 1991. Although similar in appearance to the class 465 mock-up (pictures of which were used in publicity announcing the order for the new trains), the coaches will be 23m (rather than 20m) long. Perkins engines will be fitted, probably with Voith/Gmeinder final drive which has proved successful in Provincial Sector's 'Sprinter' classes (and the Nederland Spoorwegen 'Wadloper' DHMUs where the design orginated). The Chiltern Lines version will be of 3-car formation with a maximum speed of 75mh; those on the Thames Line will be either 2- or 3-car, with a maximum speed of 90mph.

Authorisation of the first batch of 400 class 465 vehicles, to be formed into 100 4-car EMUs, was granted by Transport Secretary Cecil Parkinson on 31st August 1989. Half the £253 million order will go the newly-privatised BREL, the rest to GEC-Alstholm (formerly Metro-Cammell). Again, the trains will be much like the original models and artist's impressions, with 20m long bodyshells and a 75mph maximum speed. These will be the first of a much larger fleet to replace all the slam-door suburban stock on Kent Link and South London Lines routes. Although impressive, the specification has been trimmed down from what was promised two years earlier; there will be no air conditioning or internal information displays.

A mock-up of the proposed class 471 express 'Networker' was displayed at Victoria almost exactly two years to the day after the 465 was unveiled. These will also be 750V dc third-rail EMUs, this time to replace '4 Cep' stock on lines to the Kent Coast. Obviously sharing many design features with their suburban sisters, these units will however be able to run at up to 100mph, and have a gangwayed front end, for through passage of refreshment trolley etc. The cab end was apparently the subject of much design time and effort, but we will leave readers to judge from the photograph how successful they have been, and whether the end result is really any better than in the 'Wessex' class 442s. Internally, an entirely new design of driving cab layout is proposed. First class seating will be in compartments, but the standard class seating is the same as that in the suburban 'Networkers', including cramped 2+3 in one saloon – surely this is not good enough, however many seats the designers would like to squeeze into a train! Other new features include a telephone in the entrance vestibule and a locker built in to a luggage rack, for the carriage of Red Star parcels etc. It has not yet been decided whether or not the units will have a proper guard's van area, but it is proposed that in each 4-car unit there will be 24 first and 295 standard class seats. It is hoped that the first 45 of an intended fleet of 200 such units will enter service in 1993/94.

A list is given below of the various projected fleets of 'Networker' (electric) and 'Network Turbo' (diesel) trains now on order or proposed:

Class 165 Network Turbo
Fleet Size: 204 coaches
Train Formation: 2- or 3-car units which may be coupled in multiple.
Traction System: Diesel with 350hp engine under each vehicle.
Vehicle Length: 23 metres
Maximum Speed: 75mph on Chiltern Line, 90mph on Thames Lines
Routes: Chiltern Line from London to Aylesbury and Banbury; Thames Lines from Paddington to Reading and branches; Reading to Oxford local services; Reading to Newbury and Bedwyn.

Class 465 Networker
Fleet Size: 1000 vehicles
Train Formation: 4-car units capable of working in multiple up to 12 coaches.
Traction System: Three-phase ac electric motors with conductor rail collection from 750V dc systems.
Vehicle Length: 20 metres
Seating Capacity: 348 standard class seats in each 4-car unit, with a total carrying capacity of 1410 in a 12-car train.
Maximum Speed: 75mph
Routes: Kent Link from London (Victoria, Charing Cross, Cannon Street, Blackfriars and St Pauls) to South East London and Kent.

Class 471 Networker
Fleet Size: 800 vehicles
Train Formation: 4-car units capable of working in multiple up to 12 coaches.
Traction System: Three-phase ac traction motors working off 750V dc from conductor rail.
Vehicle Length: 20 metres
Seating Capacity: 24 first and 281 standard class in each 4-car train.
Maximum Speed: 100mph
Routes: Kent Coast from London to Maidstone, Hastings, Dover, Ramsgate etc. Eventually also Sussex Coast.

Class 331 Networker
Fleet Size: 400 vehicles.
Traction System: Three-phase ac traction motors with current collection from 25kV overhead ac.

An ac version of class 471 for London Tilbury and Southend routes from Fenchurch Street. These are projected for 1993/94 when they will be built as part of a scheme to completely renew the LT&S lines.

Class 166 Network Turbo
Fleet Size: 72 vehicles.
Traction System: Diesel, with 400hp motor under each coach.
Vehicle Length: 23 metres
Maximum Speed: 100mph

These are the proposed 'express' DMUs to replace locomotive and coach workings on Thames lines Paddington-Oxford/Newbury services.

Class 332 Networker
Fleet Size: 39 vehicles, to make 13 3-car units.
Train Formation: 3-car units, which can run in multiple to form 6-car trains.
Traction System: 3-phase AC traction motors with current collection from 25kV AC overhead.
Vehicle Length: 20 metres.
Maximum Speed: 100mph
Route: Paddington-Heathrow Airport.

This will be a small fleet of specialised EMUs to work the projected Paddington-Heathrow Airport rail link, a joint project between BAA and NSE, for which Parliamentary powers are presently being pursued. (see 'Future Developments' section) The eventual design for these units, which will be owned by Heathrow Airport Ltd, is subject to change, but they are expected to be based on the class 465.

Stations

The splendour of Imperial Baroque: the main entrance to Waterloo, designed by James Robb Scott as the 'Victory Arch' and forming the L&SWR memorial to its 585 employees killed in World War 1. It was completed in 1922. On the left, Bellona, Goddess of War; on the right, Peace enthroned on Earth, and over the cornice, Britannia holding aloft the torch of Liberty. Capital Transport

Diversity is the key word with NSE's stations. They exhibit not only characteristics of the building styles of the twelve pre-grouping companies whose lines have been inherited, but also those of the four main line companies of 1923–1947. In addition there is a surprising variety of Modernist architecture in BR's 1955–85 contribution and finally, although NSE is but three years old, it is already making its own mark with Neo-Vernacular and Post-Modernist designs. Indeed, the impact of NSE on stations is one of its chief triumphs; by the end of 1992, twenty-six new ones will have been opened since NSE's formation in 1986. Sixty rebuildings have been completed and many others have been smartened up.

Apart from age and architecture, there is also a wide spectrum of station types in the operational sense, from the great London termini and major traffic centres such as Clapham Junction, East Croydon and Reading to tiny branch line halts. Looking at the network as a whole, perhaps the most common category is the country wayside station, originating in the 19th century mostly in areas which in the last 60 years or so have become part of the outer commuter zone. Nowadays, if not rebuilt, their facilities are much scaled down: refreshment rooms, bookstalls, stationmasters, footbridge roofs and long platform canopies extending to the platform edge are mostly gone; goods yards have become car parks or have been sold for commercial or housing development. Staff, if present at all, are reduced to one or two on duty at any one time instead of half a dozen or more.

The many NSE stations with their variety of origins, design and form, almost defy description in a handbook of this size, but perhaps we can give an impression of this diversity, occasionally focussing on some individual examples.

NEW OR RE-OPENED STATIONS

1986-1989 Arlesey, Bicester Town, Corby, Haddenham & Thame Parkway, How Wood, Islip, Lake (Isle of Wight), Martin's Heron (Reading), Newbury Racecourse, Welham Green, Winnersh Triangle.

1990-1992 Cambridge Parkway, Chafford Hundred, Chaul End, Dunstable, Eastfields, Hedge End, Kidlington, Luton (Kenilworth Road), Porton, Roade, Smallbrook Interchange (Isle of Wight), St Paul's Thameslink, Stansted Airport, Thames Parkway (Iver), Totton Parkway.

Pre-grouping heritage

This is an important group, providing a tangible link with the first Railway Age. Where original buildings of some architectural interest or merit survive more or less intact they often enjoy some protection from unsympathetic alteration or destruction by inclusion on the Department of the Environment's List. Apart from the great London termini, the NSE area has a fair sprinkling of early railway architecture, much of it now carefully restored with the help of commercial sponsors or the Railway Heritage Trust. Many started life as country wayside stations, often serving quite small communities, but some larger examples also survive.

'HERITAGE' STATIONS

Anerley, Audley End, Aylesford, Barnes, Battersea Park, Battle, Blackheath, Bournemouth, Boxhill & Westhumble, Brighton, Cambridge, Canterbury West, Chertsey, Colchester St Botolphs, Culham, Cuxton, Crystal Palace, Denmark Hill, Deptford, Eastbourne, Elsenham (up platform), Etchingham, Ewell West, Fenny Stratford, Godalming, Gravesend, Great Chesterford, Greenwich, Hampton Court, Hanwell, Hertford East, Heyford, Ingatestone, Kenley, Leatherhead, Lewes, Liphook, Micheldever, Millbrook, Mortimer, North Dulwich, North Woolwich, Petersfield, Plumpton, Ridgmont, Roydon, Rye, St. Leonards (Warrior Square), Salisbury, Slough, Swaythling, Tunbridge Wells Central (up side), Wareham, Woburn Sands, Windsor & Eton (Riverside) and (Central), and Woolston.

Situated in a cutting between Leatherhead and Dorking, the little 1867 station now known as Boxhill and Westhumble owes its existence to the rigorous demands of the landowner, Thomas Grissell of nearby Norbury Park, a retired railway contractor. He not only obtained a right to have a station at which he could stop any train on request but stipulated the route of the line through his estate and required that all buildings should be of ornamental character. As to the latter, he was well served by the railway's architect, Charles Driver, who provided a main building on the down side which featured steeply-pitched roofs of patterned tiles, topped by a pyramidal turret with decorative grille and weather vane in French chateau style. Its elevations were adorned with exposed gable timbers and an imposing entrance porch with hammerbeam roof was supported by heavily decorated columns. Protecting the platform was a pretty canopy with saw-tooth conformation, each gable punctuated by a finial. The lavishly-decorated building housed a ticket hall, waiting room, lavatories and the stationmaster's residence. A small waiting room and canopy on the up platform reflected the same style.

Apart from the removal of the signal box, replacement of the canopies and removal of the footbridge roof, all the original features remain. The former stationmaster's accommodation is now used as a private residence but the little up side structure has had to be boarded up following persistent vandalism. In addition to Grissell's personal needs and those of his family and staff, this station was used by the owners and servants of two other large houses (Polesden Lacey and High Ashurst) and by inhabitants of the hamlet of Westhumble in which it stood. For many years until the 1960s, at weekends and bank holidays, it handled large numbers of South London excursionists intent on the ascent of Box Hill. Today, a fair-sized colony of mainly 1930s commuter houses of a somewhat upmarket type, hidden behind the trees on the up side, yields a daily season ticket traffic highly sensitive to the convenience of a station on its doorstep. With only one train an hour at other times, this delightful station gathers up very little or no business, especially in winter.

Gravesend, which provides a second example of this group, was built by the South Eastern Railway (SER) in 1849 on its new North Kent line to serve what was even then a quite important market town and river port. The company's architect, Samuel Beazley, contributed an impressive up side building of stock brick with stuccoed dressings, designed in simple classical style, its main elevation showing a balustraded parapet and central colonnaded recess which included the entrance from the roadway. On each side of this central block were two-storey wings, adding bulk and dignity. This range survives more or less intact in what is now a very busy station with a heavy commuter traffic and at weekends serves both up and down trains.

When it was discovered that the interior was riddled with dry rot, BR's repairs included a sympathetic and attractive refurbishment of the entrance hall and ticket office which was completed in 1983. Three years later, the exterior and approaches, including the car park, were landscaped and planted with trees, re-paved, and given a new wall and railings. These combined efforts earned a plaque for the best restored station of the year and the Brunel Award for outstanding visual design in public railway transport.

Leatherhead, LB&SCR, Up side, built in 1867 to the designs of Charles H. Driver and carefully restored by BR. Note the turret, with its herringbone frieze. Alan A. Jackson

Hatch End, L&NWR, Down Side, an elegant pavilion in red brick with Portland stone quoins much admired by the late Sir John Betjeman and designed in 1911 by Gerald Horsley, a pupil of Norman Shaw. Capital Transport

Edwardian Munificence
When new railways were built in the 1900s and 1910s, or old ones widened, everything tended to be done on a very generous scale, with no expense spared. Engineers and architects built as if railways were going on for ever as the main means of transport. New stations and most station rebuildings of this era were no exception to this trend and the NSE area can show some fine specimens: on the former South Eastern & Chatham Railway (SECR), Rochester (1908), Tunbridge Wells Central down side (1911), Dover Marine (now Western Docks) (1914-15) and Whitstable (1913/14), all by the staff architect, Alfred William Blomfield; on the former GNR, Letchworth (1913); on the LNWR widening of 1911–13, the rebuilt Harrow & Wealdstone and Hatch End, by the architect Gerald Horsley; and the stations on the Great Western's 1903–10 Direct Birmingham line between Acton and Banbury (Aynho Junction).

One of these last may be selected as an example. Bicester (now Bicester North) opened on 1st July 1910, was the second station in a small market town already served by the LNWR Oxford to Bletchley cross-country line.

As with most stations on the new GWR line, centre roads were laid for through traffic. At either side were wide granite paved platforms for the loop tracks, linked by a covered steel footbridge. The red brick buildings, single-storied and spacious in their extent, were designed by the GWR New Works Engineer, W. Armstrong. Much of the down platform was occupied by the main block, with its pitched roof extending on the railway side to form a generous canopy. This structure housed all the usual facilities as well as a refreshment room and even a changing room for those arriving by train to join the district's famous fox hunts. A small waiting room in matching style and a signal box stood on the up platform.

Much of the old atmosphere has gone: there is no longer anyone serving teas and luncheons; those coming to follow the hounds must get into their gear elsewhere; and an umbrella is needed if the footbridge has to be crossed on a rainy day. But today's Bicester does boast a taxi office, a shop and a parcels office and enough of the old survives to enable the imaginative traveller to picture the 1910s in his mind's eye.

Southern Electric Modern. J.R. Scott's design for the new Chessington branch line, Tolworth station was opened in May 1938 and seen in August 1990. Note the stark luggage lift tower on the extreme left. David Brown

Between-Wars Stations

Some very serviceable and occasionally handsome new station buildings were provided to meet special needs between the wars but the capital for them was hard-won and the list is not extensive. The LNER erected a commendably elegant and convenient station for the new Welwyn Garden City in 1926 (now being rebuilt) and in 1929 replaced the old GER structures at Clacton with a neo-Georgian brick building decorated with stone window surrounds and a stone faced central bay containing the entrance. A quadrupling and resignalling scheme between Romford and Shenfield, completed in 1934, saw dull rebuilding at Romford (1931) and substantial reconstruction at Harold Wood, Brentwood and Shenfield, the first two with four platform faces. At Shenfield, five platforms were provided, together with a new block of station offices on the west side of the line. Stratford and Maryland were extensively rebuilt for the Shenfield electrification, the former also to accommodate interchange with the Central Line eastern extensions; these works were not fully completed until 1947. Nowadays, with the Docklands Light Railway as well, Stratford is one of the most interesting traffic centres north of the Thames and is due to undergo further rebuilding.

On the Southern, the staff architect, J. Robb Scott, produced a number of good designs, firstly in the stripped Georgian popular at the time and then following up with some rather less confident essays in the Modernist style. In the first group were Ramsgate, Margate, Broadstairs and Dumpton Park, on the new Thanet lines of 1926, and Bromley North (finished in the same year), Hastings (1931) and Exeter Central (1933). All were spaciously laid out to pre-1914 standards and Hastings had some interesting art deco details. Most of the Modernist stations were in the commuter zone and included Wimbledon Chase (1929), Kingston (1935), Richmond (1937), Surbiton, Horsham, Havant and Bishopstone (all 1938), the stations on the new Chessington line (1938–39) and Woking and Swanley (both 1939). In addition there were a fair number of cheaply-built small stations, mostly for new suburban traffic and often partly-subsidised by builders and estate developers. Of this last group, Albany Park is perhaps the best example, typically forming the centrepiece of the suburb it sustained and partly paid for by New Ideal Homesteads.

The LMSR contribution to the NSE area was confined to commuter stations: those for the 1932 Barking–Upminster quadrupling and the new or rebuilt ones at Southend East (1932), South Kenton and Chalkwell (both 1933), Leigh-on-Sea and Upminster Bridge (both 1934) Elm Park and Wembley Central (both 1935), and Apsley (1938). All were designed by the company's staff architect, William H. Hamlyn, who at first favoured simple, plain brick elevations but later flirted with art deco detailing and Modernism. Wembley Central was further rebuilt by BR in 1965 and integrated into a tower block development but at street level some of Hamlyn's 1935 work remains.

From the GWR, the NSE area received nothing but six basic halts with that company's usual corrugated iron pagodas. Only three of these, South Greenford (1926), Monks Risborough (1929) and Furze Platt (1937) still survive. None retains any GWR features.

Ramsgate, a fine example of J. Robb Scott's early style, was erected on a new site, at the back of the town and a good mile from the centre, for the 1926 rationalisation of the formerly competing lines of the SER and LCDR in Thanet. Its central feature was a tall and spacious passenger hall, lit by three large round-topped windows each side which extended almost up to the cornice. This elegant plain pavilion was flanked by low wings set at an angle to it. Today the building, with its yellowish brick and stone detailing, stands handsome and dignified amidst rather undistinguished surroundings. Inside, as was usual at this period, the Engineer ruled supreme, providing workmanlike umbrella roofing over his two wide 750ft island platforms and connecting them by subways to the main concourse. A station built to handle large crowds, Ramsgate is best appreciated from its extensive forecourt.

By the end of the 1930s, following the trend established by London Transport, Scott was allowed to design the whole station as an integral unit. His four stations for the half-finished suburban loop to Leatherhead via Chessington demonstrate his use of the Modernist style and others, such as Surbiton, also show the influence of contemporary cinema architecture. In view of the expected amount of traffic from the large number of houses being built at the time around and to the south of the Kingston Bypass, it was decided to provide 541ft side platforms rather than the more economical island conformation used in many new suburban districts in the 1920s and 1930s. All were basically to the same design, but two were in brick and two in concrete.

Tolworth (1938) was one of the latter. At rail level, the dominant feature was the gracefully-curved 'Chiscarc' concrete canopies. Springing out from a back wall punctuated with steel-framed windows, these left the platform area completely unobstructed by supports and carried on their undersides an early form of fluorescent strip lighting. They were alleged to be maintenance-free but as so often in the British climate, the concrete weathered in an unattractive fashion and has had to be painted. At street level, below the railway embankment, there was a low, smoothly-curved, flat-roofed entrance block developed from a design which Scott had first tried out at Wimbledon Chase in 1929. This housed ticket and parcels offices, shop, bookstall and a ladies' room. Behind it a tower with a concrete lid accommodating the parcels and luggage lift added a necessary vertical dimension. From the roadway the appearance of the station was spoiled by ugliness in details such as the standard SR prefabricated concrete panel platform walling and the traditional style glass rooflight at the top of the staircase. Altogether it was far less successful than the contemporary stations designed for the Underground suburban extensions by Charles Holden. A five-road goods yard and shunting neck provided on the down side in 1938 survived to become a solid fuel concentration depot in 1965 and an aggregates depot in 1984.

Banbury, a GWR modernisation finally achieved by BR in 1958. The glazed section at the left shelters the main staircase to a bridge over the running lines which carries the refreshment room and other amenities. NSE

BR stations 1948–85
One of the first major BR station schemes in the NSE area was the long-delayed rebuilding of decrepit Banbury, completed in 1958. The GWR had planned a combined station for itself and the LMSR branch from Buckingham and Verney Junction, with the main building on the road bridge over the line; but this was not to be. What Banbury got instead was a somewhat insipid group of structures on the old site at the end of the approach road, serving only the former GWR line. A single storey building on the town side accommodated ticket office, concourse, left luggage counter, railway offices, staff room, and automatic telephone exchange. Joined to this and behind it, a spacious block under a sloping roof accommodated stairs rising opposite a glass wall to a 40ft wide covered bridge over the tracks. This last carried large waiting and refreshment rooms overlooking the railway and also a separate passageway with lifts for mail, luggage and parcels.

Reinforced concrete construction was used, the frame infilled with panels of London stock bricks varied with areas of tiling, glass, tyrolean rendering and concrete cladding slabs faced with Derbyshire spar chippings. All sections of the new building had central heating and fluorescent lighting. Ample concrete canopies sheltered reconstructed platforms which had bays at each end on the up side and one at the north end on the down, provision soon to be shown as excessive when Beeching closed the cross-country feeder lines. Track improvements included a new down relief loop and realignment of the main lines through the new station to allow removal of the old 60 miles an hour restriction for through trains. Certainly adequate, even generous in the sense that it was backward-looking to the old higher standards of railway provision, as architecture this was rather dull stuff.

Other major rebuildings in the NSE area, many of them associated with widenings or electrifications, were carried out at Potters Bar (1955), Cheddington (1957), Enfield Town (1958), Broxbourne (1960), Barking and Chichester (both 1961), Folkestone Central (1962), Hemel Hempstead (1964), Northampton and Bletchley (1966), Ashford Kent (1967), St Albans City (1973), and Bedford (1978). Angular and lacking in impact or imagination, with much use of tiles and plastics and large expanses of glass, occasionally relieved by areas of brick, none of these were of any great merit and many showed signs of penny-pinching. On a smaller scale, but also associated with a widening, was the new down side at St Mary Cray (1959), a station already partly rebuilt by the Southern in 1937 to meet housing development.

Other rebuildings came about when a pre-1914 station could be replaced with something meaner and easier to staff and maintain by realising the development value of the site. Railway passenger and staff facilities at ground level were then buried under many storeys of featureless office block, no longer drawing attention to their position. This sort of thing was seen at Gunnersbury (1964), Ealing Broadway (1965), Crawley and Southampton Central up side (both 1968), and Watford Junction (1985, and railside 1988). The loss of the attractive late Victorian clock tower at Southampton was particularly regrettable. At Dorking in 1982 and Henley on Thames in 1985 a rather more successful combination of offices and station was achieved.

A group of new stations arose from demands upon BR to provide facilities for the postwar New Towns, new universities and constantly-expanding airports – Gatwick Airport (1958, enlarged in 1981), Harlow Town (1960), Stevenage (1973), Basildon (1974), Moulescoomb (for Sussex University) (1980), Milton Keynes Central (1982) and Stansted Airport with a new branch line (due to open in 1991). Almost always, such provision was found to generate much new traffic. But with the exception of the last, on which judgement must be withheld, the architecture was not very exciting.

Milton Keynes, a joint project with the Development Corporation in charge of the town, incorporated a 140,000 sq ft mirror-glass six-storey office block on the east side of the line. To accommodate main line expresses, the two island platforms, and a side one on the down fast, extended to some 980ft. They were linked by a wide covered footbridge to a concourse, ticket office, shops, travel centre and buffet placed within and beneath the office block. Here at least the railway function was given some prominence in the form of a large BR double arrow logo in the window over the entrance. Within the station, decoration was confined to unimaginative ceramic tile cladding. Outside, 700 car parking spaces were laid over the fields, but the need for almost twice that number was soon evident and a multi-storey car park had to be provided. Whilst the entrance hall is not without impact, it is difficult to forgive the planners for imposing on passengers moving between buses and trains a long trek across the undoubtedly grand but bleak open forecourt.

This period was marked by sporadic and indecisive attempts to modernise inner city and suburban stations or provide new stations in these areas. No continuous programme of modernisation was apparent until the GLC started to inject initiatives and finance in the late 1970s. The 1950s saw some rather bleak and plain concrete and concrete-and-brick stations replacing outdated or war-damaged buildings or meeting the needs of increased traffic: Stonebridge Park (1948), Hampstead Heath (railside 1953, street level 1968), Twickenham and Carpenders Park (for a new GLC estate) (both 1954), Gospel Oak and Hayes, Kent (both 1955), Highbury & Islington (1956), Balham (railside only) and Willesden High Level (both 1957), West Wickham (1958), and King's Langley (1959). Wimbledon received a new entrance hall and ticket office in 1956.

The next decade saw a marked slowing down. With electrification and other modernisation activity proceeding apace, there was an evident shortage of capital for renewal of suburban and small stations. A mass of candidates for complete rebuilding went on accumulating, notably in the Southern Region. It was concluded that if the log jam was to be moved, a cheaper and faster solution than piecemeal reconstruction using traditional building methods would have to be found. In the mid-1960s the Southern Region embraced the factory parts system known as CLASP (Consortium Local Authority Special Programme), which was also used for signal cabins. This produced steel-framed single-storey boxes externally clad in precast concrete panels with exposed aggregate finish. They were unappealing, even ugly, with narrow sliding windows just below the roof line, flimsy doors with vulnerably glazed surrounds, and minimal platform canopies supported on crude-looking timber posts. Water tanks sat prominently on their flat roofs. Between 1967 and the early 1970s a rash of CLASP structures appeared, replacing decaying or war-damaged Victorian buildings at Ashtead, Belmont, Belvedere, Berrylands, Catford, Charlton, Crayford, East Grinstead, Fleet, Hampton Wick, Lower Sydenham, Slade Green, Strood and Sunbury amongst others. They have not worn well. Ashtead is now scheduled for replacement after a mere 20 years life.

Around 1973 someone had second thoughts, or perhaps the money ran out. At any rate, the CLASP programme shuddered to a stop. Fewer but more substantial and attractive reconstructions then became the order of the day. In 1974 an excellent job was done at Queens Road Peckham, where a new concrete island platform furnished with a ticket office replaced the decrepit old side platforms and ground level booking facilities. Maze Hill received an attractive glass ticket hall and entrance on the down side in 1972 and in 1975 Elmers End was given similar treatment, with the main building here on the up side of the line. At Dartford a major reconstruction, including an additional track and platform to give four running lines through the station and a glass-roofed concourse sheltering ticket office and shops, was completed in 1973-4. Funds from related property development schemes allowed improvement works to be undertaken at Sutton (1981) and Wallington (1983). Knockholt was pleasingly rebuilt in 1984 after a disastrous fire started by vandals.

Elsewhere, from 1960 onwards, there was very little activity in improving the smaller stations, apart from the GLC-inspired programme to be mentioned in a moment. 1966 saw the unavoidable rebuilding of Mill Hill Broadway, occasioned by the construction of the M1 motorway alongside the line, a project which could be funded from a less tightly-fastened public purse. Further down the same line, Radlett was reconstructed in 1979. On the Great Northern, Hatfield received a much-needed rebuilding in 1972. This took the form of a brick and timber main block on the up side, in single-storey, flat-roofed style with ugly post-supported minimal canopies. For the inner suburban electrification, Harringay and Hornsey were reprovided in a similar penny-pinching format, with platforms on the slow lines only, in 1976.

Outside inner London, only three completely new commuter type stations were added to what is now the NSE area in the whole period between the formation of BR and 1985: Hurst Green near Oxted in 1961, Garston near Watford in 1966 and Watton-at-Stone, north of Hertford, in 1982. The last two were little more than halts. Three more, Southbury, Turkey Street and Theobalds Grove, were reopened in November 1960 for the Great Eastern inner suburban electrification, after a long period of closure, using the original GER structures, suitably refurbished.

Following the entry of the GLC on to the scene in the late 1970s, a determined attack was made on the run-down stations in the inner city zone. The years 1979-86 saw complete rebuilding in substantial and attractive style of a whole batch of decaying and vandal-damaged platforms and structures including: Canning Town, Custom House and North Woolwich (all 1979), Kensal Green (1980), Kentish Town West and Blackhorse Road, with a new interchange to the Victoria Line (both 1981 – BR had wanted to close Kentish Town West after arson in 1971), Sydenham and Bush Hill Park (both 1982), Finsbury Park (main street block and ticket office, 1984, and bus interchange forecourt, 1986), Rectory Road and New Cross (both 1985), Cambridge Heath, London Fields, Crystal Palace and Abbey Wood (all 1986). Many other stations received refurbishment and partial improvements, one of the larger schemes being that at Waterloo East, finished in 1984, where in addition to repainting and tidying up the platforms, the shabby old interchange bridge to the main station was completely replaced.

In connection with the reopening of the Dalston to Stratford line and the operation of a service on to it from North Woolwich, GLC initiatives and financial assistance provided new stations at: West Ham (1979, affording interchange with District Line services), Hackney Wick and Hackney Central (1980), Dalston Kingsland (1983) and Homerton (1984). All except the first were on or near the sites of stations closed many years before.

BR neo-vernacular style at Welham Green, a new Great Northern Electric station opened in September 1986 and, in these 1990 views, somewhat swamped by oversigning at the entrance. The vandal-deterrent fencing is similar to a design adopted by the Midland Railway many years earlier. David Brown

NSE's own station programme

The impact of NSE on station expenditure has been impressive, thanks to growth in passenger revenue and use of funds obtained from property sales and redevelopments. In a few brief years we have already seen neat and sturdy new provision for the burgeoning industrial and business area between Reading and Ascot and the increasing flow of commuters into Reading: Winnersh Triangle (1986) and Martin's Heron (1988) as well as the rebuilding of Ascot (1986). For local and commuter needs, new stations have been opened (or reopened) at: Welham Green (1986), Lake (Isle of Wight), Bicester Town, Corby and Haddenham & Thame Parkway (all 1987) Arlesey, Newbury Racecourse, and How Wood (all 1988) and Islip (1989).

Major rebuilding projects have been pursued at important traffic centres used by NSE trains: Littlehampton (completed 1987), Portsmouth & Southsea High Level and King's Cross Thameslink (both 1988), Guildford and Reading (1989), Oxford and East Croydon (both 1990). Other important reconstructions have been associated with electrification, namely Weymouth, Dorchester and Poole (1986-88). A new station building at Baldock was finished in 1987. There have also been some special cases: when Eltham was relocated in 1987 and a substantial new station provided this was funded from the public purse, since two existing stations were required to close to make way for a new relief road route. Other new facilities arose from local property deals. At Epsom Downs, the tracks were cut back 300 yards and a new branch line terminus provided in 1989 to enable railway land to be profitably released for a housing development. Alongside all this, the availability of a pool of property sales income and buoyant passenger revenues have allowed continuation of the inner city renewal programme started under GLC auspices. At its best, this sort of improvement involves major clearance of redundant structures, combined with new accommodation and landscaping and tidying up what is left of the old. Brondesbury Park (1989), on which BR were advised by Brian Hodge Associates, is a fine example of this process, showing how an unpromising inner area station can be made very attractive to the passenger. Here we can see some of NSE's new station design principles in realisation. Waiting spaces and shelters are not only prominently visible (as distinct from doors off a range of platform buildings) but provide a sense of security, through good artificial lighting and all-round glazing. Staff accommodation is removed from the platforms, preferably to a location from which the platforms can be observed. Benches, shelters and lighting are solidly made, vandal-resistant without being ugly. Because the platforms are longer than normally required for today's North London Line trains, a smaller passenger area has been defined with brick paving and a circle of bollards, with the shelter as its focal point. Benches are arranged to overlook the shelter. Similar refurbishments will follow at other inner London stations in the next few years and major reconstructions are planned for Silvertown, Stratford, Highbury & Islington and Gunnersbury.

At the other end of the scale, refurbishment has for the time being had to be restricted to little more than tidying up, new lighting and repainting. Richmond showed the new NSE image for station upgrading in June 1986. The vast majority of NSE stations have received at least some smartening up, and virtually all have the famous red lamp posts. Some other changes are dictated by operating requirements: driver-only operation has brought a higher standard of lighting; and the pursuit of punctuality has led to the installation of accurate digital clocks on platforms. Platforms on the three lines to Dartford and on the main lines as far as Orpington and Sevenoaks are to be extended to take 12-car trains between now and 1993.

Thameslink has brought its own impetus to station improvement. The old City Widened Lines Metropolitan platforms at King's Cross, which had lingered on to accommodate the rush hour steam services to and from Moorgate and the Great Northern and Midland suburban lines, and latterly just the Midland diesel multiple-units, had been rebuilt for the Midland suburban electrification, becoming King's Cross Midland City in 1983. With this improvement came a spacious new concourse with a glass wall on Pentonville Road and escalators to a new pedestrian subway providing connections with the Underground and main line stations at King's Cross. Further improvements were carried out here for the Thameslink inauguration in 1988, including a transparent overall roof. Unfortunately the old platforms are much too narrow to accommodate peak hour crowds and cannot be widened without major engineering works and property demolition. It is now intended to take the Thameslink trains into the new subsurface station which it is proposed to construct beneath the King's Cross main line platforms, giving them access to the Great Northern lines as well as the Midland. Thameslink has also a new City station, St Paul's Thameslink, replacing the old Holborn Viaduct terminus, sold for office development.

Waterloo's fine curving concourse, an Edwardian design, still working well 90 years later, much brightened by BR's new barrier line (1977), white terrazzo tiling (1980-83) and the more recent NSE decor.
Capital Transport

Changes at the termini

Waterloo, the great London terminus, with its 1,200 trains and almost 200,000 passengers daily, is predominantly an NSE station. Here a long drawn-out programme of refurbishment was completed to coincide with NSE's launch on 10th June 1986. By renewing signs, lighting, barrier line and many minor structures, including shops on the concourse, and by resurfacing the concourse with white terrazzo tiling a general effect of brightness and modernity was achieved, providing an ambience reminiscent of contemporary covered shopping malls. This contributes positively to the image the railway projects to its passengers – now known as 'customers' in extension of the modern retailing comparison. Much of this work at Waterloo was done before NSE was born, but it all came together under the NSE banner, making a powerful impact, both on the public and on the advertisers who use the station.

The treatment was carried down to the Waterloo & City tube platforms below, and the new, clean and bright style of décor was adopted for other important central area stations used by NSE, notably King's Cross Suburban (where a third platform was provided in 1989), Euston's NSE platforms, Victoria, Charing Cross and Fenchurch Street.

Most London termini used predominantly or entirely by NSE have undergone more or less major rebuildings since the 1950s. At Cannon Street work started in 1955 but was not finished until 1974 and reconstruction of Blackfriars was completed in 1979. A much-needed rearrangement and almost total reconstruction of London Bridge was finished in 1979, providing a station far more convenient to use than the old one but leaving the old LBSCR overall roof. At Fenchurch Street, an office development over the station provided a bright new entrance and concourse, finished in 1987, and retaining the old street façade. Now further work is proceeding here as another office development rises over the outer end of the platforms. In 1989 Charing Cross gained a refurbished concourse, new ticket and travel offices and entrances but work in the platform area, the new office block above and the forecourt is still proceeding at the time of writing. Victoria has been under reconstruction for a long period to accommodate office blocks, new taxi, car and parcels facilities and shopping areas over the platforms; work is still going on, although the enlarged concourses and rebuilt and rearranged platforms are virtually finished. Finally, at Liverpool Street, a massive and total rebuilding is under way, providing a new concourse and passenger amenities as part of a development scheme involving a whole complex of office and shopping developments, some of which are already finished.

Above **The handsome Hertford East, of 1888, with its impressive *portes cochères*. The GER architect, W.N. Ashbee, succeeded well in providing appropriate dignity for the county town (the GNR station was less impressive).** NSE

Left **The Victorian GWR's solution to the problem of designing a station on an embankment, employing a standardised pattern; Hanwell, as rebuilt in 1877.** Capital Transport

Deep in the Buckinghamshire countryside at Little Kimble there are but 11 trains each way daily and a mere handful of passengers. With one short, curving platform, modest station house with prettily-valanced canopy, and its single track, Little Kimble looks very much as it did when opened by the GWR in 1872 — apart of course from those red lamp posts. NSE

Top **Faversham exhibits the fairly standardised LC&DR architectural style. Opened in 1858, it was refurbished by NSE in 1988.** NSE

Above **GNR suburban style at Palmers Green, a station built in 1871 and little altered, although the elaborate bargeboards and finials were sadly allowed to rot away.** David Brown

Left **In 1912-13 the Down side of Tunbridge Wells was rebuilt to the plans of the SE&CR's architect, Alfred William Blomfield. He provided an impressive Imperial Baroque block for the street frontage in the main part of the town, seen towering above more recent additions.** Barry Coward

Gravesend Up side, as designed for the SER by Samuel Beazley in 1849 and magnificently restored by BR in 1985. R.C. Riley

William Tress's little Tudoresque 1851 station at Frant at the time electrification reached it in April 1986. Alan A. Jackson

Purley Up side in August 1990, as rebuilt in 1899 by the LB&SCR following the quadrupling of the Brighton main line between South Croydon and Coulsdon North. It is typical of the lavish passenger amenity provision of this pre-grouping company.
Alex Dasi-Sutton

Above **Bexley, an enduring example of the many SER clapboarded wayside stations. It was opened with the Dartford Loop line in September 1866.**
Alan A. Jackson

GER suburban: Walthamstow Central, opened in April 1870 as Hoe Street, it still exhibits in the electrification age its original pointed arch windows, saw-tooth canopies and elaborate valancing.
Alan A. Jackson

Dormans: an LB&SCR country wayside station, in the style of 1884. This rural scene shows little change in over 100 years. Electrification reached the line to East Grinstead in 1987. Alan A. Jackson

J. Robb Scott's spacious 1926 station for Ramsgate, built for the crowds of holidaymakers which faded away after 30 years or so. Its classical dignity was still potent when these photos were taken in more recent times. NSE

At Bromley North in 1926 this elegant neo-Georgian pavilion by J.R. Scott replaced the tatty wooden shed provided by the SER. Unfortunately it is now somewhat overwhelmed by an ugly 1970s tower block which this photo mercifully excludes. R.C. Riley

L&NER neo-Georgian at Clacton, where the station was completely rebuilt in 1930. This 1990 view shows the building after the recent BR refurbishment. Similarity with Scott's contemporary work on the Southern is apparent, but it seems slightly second rate in comparison. The impoverished L&NER, unlike the other three members of the 'Big Four', did not employ a staff architect (except in former NER territory), nor did it go to a well-known name outside on the few occasions when it built new. NSE

Another J.R. Scott neo-Georgian design for the early years of the Southern Electric: the rebuilt Sutton of 1925. The chimney detailing is particularly pleasing. A busy and well-sited station, it is seen here in January 1990. Alan A. Jackson

Hanwell, looking to London. The buildings are typical GWR designs of their period (1877), though the end patterns of the platform structures were varied and here an attractive 'pointed arch' effect was produced. This station was refurbished by BR in Victorian style in 1981, retaining GWR nameboards and fitted out with 'electrified' gas lamp standards. Capital Transport

Warnham, a typical LB&SCR wayside country station of 1867, incorporating stationmaster's house and virtually unaltered in this photo of June 1988. The standard small LB&SCR/Saxby & Farmer signal box at the left dates from 1877. Alan A. Jackson

Temporary platforms had been provided for the new Letchworth Garden City in 1903 but this rather heavy-handed attempt at a quasi-domestic style to tone in with the surroundings did not appear until 1913. It was probably designed in the GNR Engineer's Office. At rail level, provision was made for two island platforms and four tracks; two luggage lift towers adjoined the covered footbridge. This 1990 photo shows virtually no change to the 1913 elevations. David Brown

Albany Park, one of a series of SR stations erected to serve new suburban housing estates between the wars and partly subsidised by the house builders, in this case New Ideal Homesteads Ltd. A covered and glazed footbridge was provided but the platform structures were cheaply-built, largely in wood. This view looks towards London. Alan A. Jackson

Apsley, one of the few new suburban stations built in the London area by the LM&SR, dates from September 1938. The company's architect, William H. Hamlyn, had obviously been studying the contemporary Holden architecture on the Underground. NSE

Another Hamlyn design, the new Chalkwell station opened in September 1933 between Leigh-on-Sea and Westcliff. The assymetrical position of the rather ineffective feature above the cornice suggests that the original plans were for a larger building. John Reed

Scott's Chessington line designs were the Southern's first fully-integrated stations in the Modern style, as this 1990 picture of the 1938 Tolworth demonstrates. Beneath the 'Chisarc' reinforced concrete canopies was fluorescent strip lighting, a very early example of the use of this feature in a public building. David Brown

The main building of the new Bedford station was completed by BR in 1978, but the platform reconstruction and rearrangement was not finished until 1981. This was an early example of the use of the Post-Modern style for a British railway station, exemplified by the exposed structural steelwork in its large square concourse, some of which can be seen through the windows in this 1990 platform view. NSE

Southern Region rebuilt Queens Road Peckham in 1974, providing a new concrete island platform with ticket office and waiting shelter to replace the wooden side platforms and structures and street level booking office, all of which had reached an advanced stage of decrepitude. Alan A. Jackson

The Pentonville Road façade of King's Cross Thameslink in 1990. This station represented a thorough reconstruction of the old Widened Lines platforms (east of the 1941 Metropolitan and Circle station), first in 1977-78 for the Midland Electrics and then again, ten years later, for Thameslink services. NSE

Station-cum-office block. The building at Milton Keynes was completed in 1982 as a joint project with the Milton Keynes Development Corporation. The entrance, seen here, is within a large but totally uninteresting office complex and is dominated by an oversize BR symbol. NSE

Watford Junction is another example of a station within an office block, but in this case a rebuilding, completed in 1988, on the site of an existing station to maximise the return from BR-owned land. Whilst this process brings in useful capital which can be spent on improving railway infrastructure, it neutralises the image a railway station presents to the street; the NSE frieze and freestanding BR symbol seen in this 1990 view are the only indications of what lies beyond. Capital Transport

The glitzy interior of the 1988 King's Cross Thameslink with narrow platforms and mirror glass used to give an illusion of spaciousness. This station, seen here in 1990, has to handle virtually all the suburban traffic once using St Pancras as well as Thameslink. Inevitably, it must soon be rebuilt again, as part of the planned reconstruction and enlargement of King's Cross. Capital Transport

More Post-Modernism. The rebuilt Weymouth terminus, designed for its new electric services, seen here soon after completion in 1986. Note the small echo of the glass pyramid at les Invalides in Paris. BR (Southern)

And now for something completely different . . . the rebuilt Epsom Downs terminus, erected in 1989 in a new Charles Church housing estate and made to look as much as possible like its surroundings with an 'add-on' railway character. Beyond, there is but a single track and one side platform. The pillars supporting the valanced canopy were rescued from the old terminus. David Brown

Brondesbury Park, thoroughly refurbished in 1989 as a prototype for improving shabby inner area NSE stations. Note the clock on the bridge and the high-visibility waiting areas, designed to deter vandalism and mugging. NSE

An architectural drawing of the new Liverpool Street West Side and the refurbished Great Eastern Hotel. This huge project, which involved total reconstruction of one of London's largest and busiest stations whilst it continued in full railway use, is due for completion in 1991. NSE

Southern Electric in suburbia: Class 451/1 4-EPB set 5202 leaves Crofton Park. Brian Morrison

Electrification Systems

The greater part of Network SouthEast's passenger services are now electrically-worked and further lines are scheduled for conversion in the next decade. In this section we briefly survey the history of the six main groups of electric lines.

SOUTHERN ELECTRIC (Kent Link; South London Lines, South Western Lines; Kent Coast; Sussex Coast; Portsmouth Line; Wessex Electrics and Island Line).
The extensive Southern Electric network was for many years the largest mileage of electrified railway in Britain. Its origins go back to the London, Brighton and South Coast Railway (LBSCR), which had gained powers to electrify all its lines in 1903 under threat from rival (but in the event, stillborn) schemes for an electric railway between London and Brighton. The Company was also seeking to reduce the cost of operating its declining suburban operations, and electrification seemed one answer. The first route converted was the South London line from Victoria to London Bridge via Peckham Rye (passenger bookings at Peckham Rye had fallen from 1.2m in 1902 to 0.5m in 1909). Electrification was a financial success, regaining lost revenue, and conversion of the routes from Victoria and London Bridge to Crystal Palace (low level) and Norwood Junction followed in 1911-1912. Work on further extensions was halted by the outbreak of the first world war, as equipment could not be obtained from its German makers – but electrification on the LBSCR system to Coulsdon and Sutton was finally brought into use by the Southern Railway in 1925.

The system adopted was single phase ac with a traction current of 6700V 25Hz carried to the motor cars via catenary overhead wires and bow collectors, a somewhat bold choice at the decision time (1904) given the state of development of single phase series traction motors, but influenced by a long term requirement for electric main line services.

More important for the future however were the London & South Western Railway (LSWR) suburban electrifications of 1915-16 (Waterloo – East Putney – Wimbledon; Kingston and Hounslow services; Shepperton and Hampton Court services; Surbiton – Claygate). These were a response to competition from the London United electric tramways and threats of tube railway extensions into its lush Thames Valley commuter territory. (The combined efforts of the new motor buses and tramways with their through fares to the electrified District Railway were robbing the LSWR of a million passengers a year by 1913). Here the choice was fairly straightforward since an economical, efficient and reliable system for suburban working was all that was required and compatibility with District Railway electric trains, already running over LSWR tracks to Wimbledon and Richmond, was important. The choice therefore fell upon the USA tried and tested 600/660V dc third rail. Largely through a general conviction of its success and suitability for suburban working on the part of Herbert Walker (the LSWR's and subsequently Southern Railway's general manager), it was this system which was adopted for the electrification of the greater part of the Southern's London suburban network in the years 1925-32, including conversion of the ex-LBSCR overhead ac lines.

Electric working proved a commercial success for the SR, a particularly gratifying feature being the generation of a healthy off-peak traffic. This led the company to embark on conversion of the coastal services, beginning with those to Brighton and Worthing in 1932-33, using the same third rail dc system. In essence this was simply a projection of the London suburban network, using similar equipment and basic principles and the traffic handled was of a similar nature, containing as it did a significant proportion of daily commuters and day return passengers. Main line electric working proper in the NSE area may be said to have begun in 1937 with the conversion of the direct Portsmouth services, but even here a heavy daily residential traffic was carried, much of it lucrative First Class business from stations such as Haslemere and Guildford. The SR continued filling in the gaps in its London suburban and outer area electrified network until the second world war called a halt. By 1939, its third rail dc electric trains were in Kent, serving Maidstone, Sevenoaks and the Medway Towns, as well as most of the important traffic centres and lines in Sussex, nearly all in Surrey and into much of north east Hampshire. Heavy traffic to and from the military and naval centres at Aldershot, Portsmouth and Chatham was to benefit from these new electric services in wartime. In this last period of Southern Railway enterprise, two entirely new suburban electric railways were constructed: from Wimbledon to Sutton in 1929-30; and from Motspur Park to Chessington South in 1938-39, both penetrating areas where hundreds of new houses were being erected by speculative builders and the first also serving a vast new estate of the London County Council. However the planned completion of the Chessington line as a relief loop, returning to the existing railway just north of Leatherhead, was stifled by post-war planning legislation which restricted London's outward growth.

British Railways further extended the Southern Electric, employing the same basic system of current supply and working. In general, the BR schemes have included modernisation of signalling and other fixed equipment, which was by no means always the case with the earlier Southern work. BR began with the important Kent Coast electrifications, completed in two stages, in June 1959 and June and October 1961. By the latter date, all the remaining passenger lines in Kent were electrified, apart from three short sections, one of which has been subsequently converted, and Ashford to Hastings. July 1967 saw full electric working along the old LSWR main line from Woking to Basingstoke, Southampton and Bournemouth, together with the branch to Lymington Pier, whilst in March the same year the last remnant of the Isle of Wight Railways (Ryde to Shanklin) was saved from closure by low-cost electrification using secondhand trains from the London deep level tube railways.

In May 1986, nearly 20 years since the previous conversion, the long-planned electrification of the Hastings direct line from Tonbridge at last became a reality, track singling and re-signalling through the restricted loading gauge tunnels making it possible to avoid the cost of special rolling stock. Another long-standing omission was corrected in October 1987 when the outer suburban line from South Croydon through Oxted to East Grinstead was converted. In October of the following year, electric working was extended from Bournemouth to Dorchester and Weymouth (excluding the Harbour Tramway), carrying the Southern Electric, still basically in its 1915 LSWR suburban format, to its westernmost point, 142 miles from London.

The original LSWR and SR suburban schemes were supplied with electricity from railway-owned generating stations (the chimneys of the LSWR installation at Durnsford Road were a familar landmark on the Wimbledon skyline for many years), fed to the trains at 600/660V dc via rotary converter substations, which had to be manned continuously. The south coast and suburban extensions of the 1930s however were supplied with three phase power from the National Grid via unmanned rectifier substations, centrally monitored from control rooms (such as that at Three Bridges on the Brighton main line). These substations were housed in distinctive lineside buildings either in brick or faced with the ubiquitous SR concrete, with the switchgear mounted outside on concrete frames. The substations on a route were connected by cabling at line voltage, and between each pair was a track paralleling (TP) hut, containing switchgear to isolate any substation in the event of a malfunction. In an emergency, any two substations could do the work of three.

Similar arrangements were used for the BR Kent Coast electrifications, except that one substation (Hollingbourne on the Maidstone East – Ashford route) was experimentally equipped with silicon-diode semi-conductor rectifiers in place of the mercury-arc devices used latterly by the SR. All subsequent Southern Region electrifications have utilised semi-conductor rectifiers, which have also now replaced all the mercury-arcs in older installations. A scheme to modernise the power supply arrangements on the suburban lines was also carried out in the late 1950s, doing away with the obsolete and expensive-to-run rotary converters and private generating stations, all electricity requirements now coming from the Grid (of which BR is the largest customer). Since 1983 all lines have used the higher traction voltage of 750, made possible by the withdrawal of the last suburban rolling stock

The modern Southern Electric: Permanent way, conductor rail arrangement and substation at Etchingham on the Tonbridge-Hastings electrification of 1986. BR (Southern)

built to pre-war specifications (the 4 SUBs). The 1967 Bournemouth line electrification was given rather unsightly steel-clad substation buildings, but those for the 1986 Hastings via Tonbridge scheme were housed in pleasant brick 'chalet' style huts. The TP huts, however, were factory-assembled in modular form for simple installation on site, and these arrangements were extended to include the substations as well in the East Grinstead, Weymouth and Southampton – Portsmouth schemes. All electrifications since Hastings via Tonbridge have been supplied from the Grid at 11kV rather than the standard 33kV, reducing cost but placing limitations on the number and length of trains which can be operated (for example, through Waterloo – Weymouth trains may normally be formed of only five cars west of Poole). This is now seen as a false economy, and there are plans to boost the supply on the Bournemouth – Weymouth route.

Distance between substations may be as close as under one mile in the busy inner areas, but in the countryside spacings extend up to five miles. Current is passed between substations and to the conductor rail through oil-filled cables. The oil reservoirs are also a distinctive lineside feature of SR electric lines, generally mounted in concrete troughing, although plastic was experimentally used in places on the Hastings line. On the track itself, the conductor rail is mounted on porcelain insulators (or 'pots') mounted outside the running rails; current passes to the trains' motors via cast iron shoes and then returns to the substation through the wheels after it has energised the motors. The conductor rail is of high-conductivity steel, but aluminium rail has been experimentally installed between Fareham and Botley.

Electrification of the important south east Hampshire links between Eastleigh / Southampton and Portsmouth, ready early in 1990, is likely to be followed by conversion of the valuable cross country route from Reading via Guildford and Dorking to Redhill (whence most trains run on over the existing electric lines to Gatwick Airport) and Tonbridge. When that is completed, electric trains will serve every passenger line in Surrey, a county which interestingly retains almost all the railways it has ever had, despite some of the highest car ownership in Britain. NSE is also hoping to electrify Ashford to Hastings; Hurst Green to Uckfield; and Reading to Basingstoke.

NORTH LONDON LINES

For many years, the London & North Western Railway (LNWR) neglected the development of a London suburban business, seeing this as unlikely to become particularly remunerative and resting content with the satisfactory profits reaped from its long-distance freight and passenger traffic. This attitude was modified in the early 1900s when new deep level electric tube railways were being proposed and constructed at the same time as street tramways were undergoing extension and electrification. In 1906 the LNWR board approved a scheme for a new pair of electrically-worked suburban tracks alongside the existing lines between Euston and Watford, to terminate in a deep level tube loop at the inner end.

Even more serious than the perceived threat to the LNWR's potential suburban traffic was the effect the new competitors were having on the North London Railway (NLR), especially its services between Richmond, Willesden and its City terminus at Broad Street. In 1908 the NLR lost over 3.5m passengers (excluding season ticket holders) against the previous year, which in its turn had yielded over 3m fewer than 1906; in all, between 1902 and 1908, the seepage totalled 10.2m. The company was forced to reduce fares and its dire situation eventually led to its working being taken over by the LNWR in February 1909. On its own, the NLR had no hope of raising capital for the electrification which had been considered in 1904 and again in 1908, but the LNWR was of course in a better position to do so and 1911 modified its own scheme to include the western lines of the NLR as well as a projection of Bakerloo tube over its proposed new suburban line as far as Watford. Sharing of Richmond-Gunnersbury with District electric trains and running of Bakerloo tube trains over

Queen's Park to Watford section dictated the choice of system: 630V dc with positive and negative return rails. In recent years, this has been modified. Since the Bakerloo trains ceased to run between Harrow & Wealdstone and Watford in the early 1980s, only the section between the former and Queen's Park is now operated on the conventional '4-rail' system as used on the Underground and even on this BR trains now use only the third rail. In 1966 the section between Turnham Green, Gunnersbury and Richmond, shared with District Line trains, was modified with a centre rail that merely served as a contact for the Underground trains' negative shoes; no longer an insulated return, the centre rail was bonded to the running rails, which acted as conductors for the return current. This arrangement, which still applies, is very similar to that which has always been used on the East Putney and Wimbledon line, shared by the Southern Electric and District trains.

A full, all-day electric timetable between Broad Street and Watford Junction became operative on 10th July 1922. On that day LNWR electrics also began to provide the Euston – Watford Junction stopping services, supplementing the Baker-loo trains which had been running out to Watford since April 1917. At the outer end of the LNWR electric system, the trains used the tracks from Bushey to Watford High Street which had been completed in 1913 and initially steam-worked. The Croxley Green – Watford High Street line, opened for steam in 1912, received its electric trains on 30th October 1922. The eastern section of the old North London Railway, which had lost its steam passenger services in 1944, was brought back to life between 1979 and 1985 and linked to a piece of the old Great Eastern system, following initiatives and financial assistance from the former Greater London Council (GLC), which was seeking to improve access to the redeveloped Docklands and inner city decay in north east London in the hope of attracting new development opportunities. As a start, a DMU service had been introduced between North Woolwich and Camden Road on 14th April 1979, though work on the new and rebuilt stations along this route was not completed until 1985. With a GLC grant, BR was able to extend third rail dc electric working over the 8.5 miles between Dalston and North Woolwich from 13th May 1985, providing a basic service every twenty minutes, seven days a week, between North Woolwich and Richmond. This left the Broad Street City terminus and its approaches from Dalston Junction accommodating only the residual Monday to Friday peak hour workings to and from Watford Junction. With the complete closure of Broad Street station for commercial redevelopment of the site after traffic on 27th June 1986, these rush hour trains were diverted into Liverpool Street station over a new connecting curve at Hackney Downs. This service, starting on 30th June 1986, required dual-fitted stock since the curve and tracks thence into Liverpool Street were electrified on the 25kV 50Hz ac overhead line system.

Also included in the NSE North London Lines is the former LNWR single track branch from Watford Junction to St Albans, which has been electrically worked on the 25kV 50Hz ac system since 11th July 1988. With its unmanned stopping places, fare collection on the train and simple catenary overhead, this is at present very reminiscent of an electric light railway. But its importance may soon increase: suggestions have been made, though not by NSE, that it might form part of a new orbital route linking the main station in St Albans with Watford, Rickmansworth and Chesham. This would involve very little new construction and might be financed from the sale of released railway land in St Albans and Watford which has a high commercial value. There are also plans for some through workings to central London.

NSE is proposing to extend the North London electrified network by electrifying the orbital link between Gospel Oak, South Tottenham and Barking, at present worked by DMUs. A very small part of this, through South Tottenham station, was equipped with 25kV 50Hz overhead line in 1989 to provide a link between Seven Sisters and the Lea Valley/Stratford lines, so it seems likely this system will be used.

Northampton Line Electrics: class 321 321421 leaving Euston with a train to Northampton in April 1990. The massive overhead work of the 1965 LMR electrification shows up well in this picture. Chris Wilson

NORTHAMPTON LINE

In addition to the North London Lines services out of Euston, there are outer-suburban and medium-distance electric NSE trains to Northampton via the ten intermediate stations on the main line north of Watford, including that opened in May 1982 for the new town of Milton Keynes. These services date back to the 25kV 50Hz overhead wire electrification of the London Midland Region main line. Starting between November 1965 and January 1966 with excellent new multiple unit stock, they replaced an unattractive, irregular and infrequent steam (and, briefly, diesel-hauled) service, soon building up a healthy new business.

During the 1980s, to meet increasing traffic at Northampton and the outer area stations (including a 40 per cent growth in commuters in 1986-88), there were timetable and capacity improvements and plans for a new station at Roade.

The Northampton Line is linked at Bletchley with the electrified Midland's outer terminus at Bedford by a DMU service which calls at no fewer than ten intermediate stations, some of them in the brickmaking industrial area near Bedford. NSE is hoping to convert this route to 25kV 50Hz electric working before the end of 1992, a remarkable turn-round for a line that BR was proposing to close as recently as 1972.

Although Euston – Northampton was not the first use of the now standard BR ac overhead line system in the NSE area (Colchester – Clacton/Walton had been so electrified in 1959) it is convenient to outline the fixed equipment details here. Power is taken from the National Grid, generally at 132kV via Grid substations which step it down to 25kV. It is then cabled to railside feeder stations spaced on average 20-30 miles apart, from which it passes through circuit breakers to the overhead wires which supply the trains and locomotives through their pantograph collectors. Various arrangements of suspension and support are used but always there is a contact wire attached to droppers hanging from a second wire known as the catenary. The catenary, which is fastened by insulators to the gantry or bracket supports, shows a considerable sag in the stretches between the supports and carries much of the traction current. It is tensioned by weights at the end of each length of up to 6000ft. Originally lattice steel portals were used to support the wires on four track sections but current practice is to install headspan construction, between galvanised steel masts. On double track sections, BR now employs separate masts for each track, each set supporting catenary for its side and these single track masts and cantilevers are also installed for a single track electrification. Overhead line structures are bonded to a running rail and an insulated path for the return traction current is provided by a return conductor near the top of the mast, the current encouraged on its way by booster transformers mounted on the overhead masts at about two-mile intervals to produce a difference in potential.

Originally the voltage was lowered to 6.25kV in some heavily built-up areas (but not on the Northampton Line), to reduce the civil engineering costs of rebuilding bridges and tunnels to provide the necessary safe clearances, but subsequent experience has shown this to be unnecessary and all the 6.25kV sections had been converted to the standard 25kV by 1989, the London, Tilbury & Southend being the last.

LONDON-BEDFORD (part of Thameslink)
From January 1960 until March 1983 the former Midland Railway and LMSR suburban services from St Pancras and Moorgate to St Albans, Luton and Bedford were operated entirely by diesel multiple units. These diesel operated services were claimed, probably correctly, as the most intensive of their kind in the world. New traffic was generated, growing by at least one fifth over the total carried by the steam trains, and with continuing housing development along the line, and diesel trains on their last legs, it was possible to make out a strong case for electrification. This was accepted and installed on the now standard BR system of 25kV 50Hz ac with overhead catenary, but the start of the new services, with their associated track changes and complete resignalling, was delayed by an industrial dispute on the single-manning which BR was to introduce as part of the financial package. Test running of the new stock was thus inhibited and when a mixed service of the old DMUs and the new electrics began on 28th March 1983 it soon became apparent that the latter required modifications. It was not until 23rd January 1984, two years after the planned start date, that it proved possible to operate full electric working. After that things went smoothly, the comfortable and very fast new trains building up a substantial new traffic, despite the infelicitous tag the *Bed*(ford)*pan*(cras) line, now mercifully consigned to oblivion by subsequent changes.

As part of this scheme, most of the trains were diverted from St Pancras to Moorgate, calling at King's Cross Midland (now King's Cross Thameslink), the former Metropolitan Railway City Widened Lines stations, enlarged and modernised.

Following a GLC-financed feasibility study, the service was again reorganised to provide the Thameslink north-south connection via Farringdon and Blackfriars on 16th May 1988. This imaginative scheme, involving relaying track in a tunnel not used throughout for regular passenger trains since 1908, diverted the majority of the Midland line suburban services though central London to East Croydon, Gatwick and Brighton; to Sevenoaks via Orpington and via Otford; and, at certain times of the day, to Wimbledon via Streatham with connections at Tulse Hill at other times. Signalling changes have allowed increased frequency on the central section and in May 1990 this useful and increasingly patronised cross-city link was further improved, to serve Epsom and Guildford. Dual-fitted rolling stock is used and the changeover from 25kV 50Hz ac overhead to 750V dc third rail is made during a slightly extended stop at Farringdon station.

GREAT NORTHERN

Great Northern suburban services have a long history going back to the early 1870s, related to the construction or branches into districts such as Enfield, Highgate and Finchley which were capable of generating commuter housing development, and to opening of new stations on the main line to serve similar areas. Well before 1914, this traffic was heavy, despite the diversion of part of the load over the North London lines into Broad Street via Canonbury after January 1875. The GNR considered electrification, as did the impoverished LNER, which was unable to raise the necessary capital. Between the wars, Government financial assistance first favoured an Underground extension to Southgate and Cockfosters in 1932-3, penetrating what had been exclusively Great Northern territory, a development which soon drew off traffic from the half a dozen inner area stations on the main and Hertford loop lines. Then, in 1939-41, with LNER participation, the Northern Line of the Underground was projected over the former GNR 'Northern Heights' lines, tube trains running out to Finchley, High Barnet and Mill Hill East.

With post-war population and industrial growths at Hatfield, Welwyn and Stevennage, outer suburban electrification became an increasingly attractive proposition and since this would entail modernisation of fixed equipment, it was logical to include the remaining inner suburban services in any scheme. The work done in 1959 to quadruple the main line bottleneck between New Barnet (Greenwood) and Potters Bar, including rebuilding of the station at the latter point, was a useful preliminary to any intensification of suburban services. Operation of suburban trains into King's Cross, Moorgate and Broad Street by diesel multiple units, or with diesel locomotive haulage, which started in 1958-59, could be regarded as no more than a stop-gap, its effectiveness hampered by the retention of the outdated semaphore signalling.

Following the announcement of Great Northern suburban electrification in 1971, BR set about construction of what was virtually a new railway, with rebuilt tracks, new layouts and bridges, signalling modernisation and some station rebuilding. Overhead line equipment supplying 25kV ac 50Hz was installed over the 67.3 route miles from King's Cross and Drayton Park to Royston, via Hatfield and via Hertford North. Included in the scheme was a physical link with the 1902 main-line loading-gauge Great Northern & City tube railway, which had originally been planned with just such a connection in mind. Owing to the restricted clearances on the 2.73m deep-level tube section into Moorgate, the Great Northern Electrics, as they came to be called, were to operate over this on 750V dc third rail, the changeover effected during the stop at Drayton Park station. Inner suburban services to Welwyn Garden City and Hertford North, using dual-fitted trains, began on 8th November 1976.

A partial outer suburban service to Welwyn Garden City, Hitchin, Letchworth and Royston was started on 3rd October 1977 but the full timetable did not come into operation until 6th July 1978. Finally, the Hertford North – Stevenage line was electrically-worked from 14th May 1979. Encouraged by electrification, traffic built up impressively. Watton-at-Stone station, north of Hertford, was reopened in 1982 and on 29th September 1986 an entirely new station was provided at Welham Green, just south of Hatfield with platforms serving the two outside tracks used by the inner suburban electrics.

For a few more years passengers travelling from London to Cambridge via Hitchin were obliged to change from electric multiple units to diesel cars at Royston, usually by walking further along the same platform, but this ceased in May 1988 when electric trains began to run between Royston and Cambridge. Completion of this 'missing link', with the associated faster trains, has made this the most popular of the two alternative rail routes between the university town and the capital.

Electrification of the main line from King's Cross to Leeds and Edinburgh, planned as long ago as 1955, was finally started thirty years later. This has brought further projection of the 25kV ac 50Hz services, to Huntingdon and Peterborough.

Stratford, looking to Liverpool Street: five different electrification systems have been used or are in use in this area: 1500 V dc overhead; 6.25 and 25kV ac overhead; 660V dc third and fourth rail (London Underground); and 750V third rail (DLR), but in this view the ac overhead prevails, indeed dominates the scene. NSE

Anglia Electrics: Unit 315857 arriving at Bethnal Green with the 08.57 Chingford-Liverpool Street train in April 1989. The use of a telephoto lens emphasises the mass of steelwork used in this, one of the earliest (1960) BR ac electrification schemes. Chris Wilson

Below **Great Northern Electrics:** Unit 313061 on a Welwyn Garden City-Moorgate stopping train in August 1990. The lighter overhead adopted for more recent ac electrification is well apparent. David Brown

ANGLIA ELECTRICS AND LONDON TILBURY & SOUTHEND

Electric working of the heavily-patronised and intensively-worked steam suburban services of the old Great Eastern Railway (GER) and of the whole of the busy London Tilbury & Southend Railway (LTSR), with its considerable commuter and pleasure traffic, was proposed in the 1900s but apart from one small exception, had to wait until 1949-62 before being achieved. The Midland Railway, on taking over the LTSR in 1912, had given a solemn undertaking to electrify, and although neither it nor its successor the LMSR was able to fulfil this, the latter did agree to the extension of District Line trains from Barking to Upminster in 1932, providing two additional tracks and some new station accommodation. In the relevant legislation, a release was given from the earlier obligation.

Electrification of the old GER main line as far as Shenfield, integrated with extension of Central Line tube trains over former GER suburban lines to Loughton and Epping and around the Fairlop/Hainault Loop, was achieved as part of the great 1935-40 London Railways New Works Programme. In November 1949 a full 1500V dc overhead line multiple unit service came into operation between Liverpool Street, Ilford, Romford and Shenfield. At the same time, the tracks between Stratford and Fenchurch Street were wired, and although the original intention of providing a shuttle service between these two points was never realised, the facility proved useful for emergency diversions and stock transfers. Electric services were extended to Chelmsford in June and to Southend (Victoria) in December 1956. All these lines were converted to the new standard 50Hz ac system in 1960-61.

Further extension of electric working along the main line and its branches followed: Colchester-Clacton/Walton in 1959; Chelmsford to Colchester in 1962 (Full electric services between London and Clacton/Walton began in June 1963); Witham to Braintree in 1977; Colchester to Manningtree in 1985; and Manningtree to Harwich, Romford to Upminster, and Wickford to Southminster in 1986.

Decisions to electrify at long last the old GER inner suburban lines from Liverpool Street to Enfield Town, Walthamstow and Chingford and also the former GER lines to Bishop's Stortford and Hertford East and the LTSR lines, were announced as part of the British Railways Modernisation Plan of 1955. All were to use the overhead line 50Hz ac system. The scheme included a reopening of the loop line between Edmonton and Cheshunt to provide the electric route to Hertford East and Bishop's Stortford. This had been closed to passengers between 1909 and 1915 and since 1919, but all three intermediate stations were now refurbished and reopened. Broxbourne station was also completely rebuilt for the electric services, which began between Liverpool Street, Enfield Town, Chingford, Hertford East and Bishop's Stortford on 21st November 1960. Alas, there were serious technical difficulties in working with new 6.25kV multiple unit stock, making it impossible to operate the full planned services until 18th June 1962.

Electrification of the Lea Valley line between Cheshunt and Clapton was completed in 1969, providing two routes as far out as Cheshunt. Finally electric working was extended from Bishop's Stortford to Cambridge in May 1987 and completion as far as the NSE boundary at King's Lynn is currently in progress, together with a new electrified branch to serve Stansted Airport, due to open in 1991.

Almost exactly fifty years elapsed between the time when electrification of the LTSR services between Fenchurch Street and Southend and Shoeburyness via Upminster and via Tilbury was thought to be a high priority and its realisation. In June 1962 the full timetable was inaugurated on both routes, using the now standard 50Hz ac overhead wire system and replacing an appallingly poor steam service. Barking station, an important interchange point, was rebuilt at the same time and two new flyovers and a dive-under were provided here to eliminate conflicting movements by freight and make things easier for passengers changing to and from the Underground services. To complete the scheme, the cross-country loop from Upminster to Grays received an electric service from June 1963.

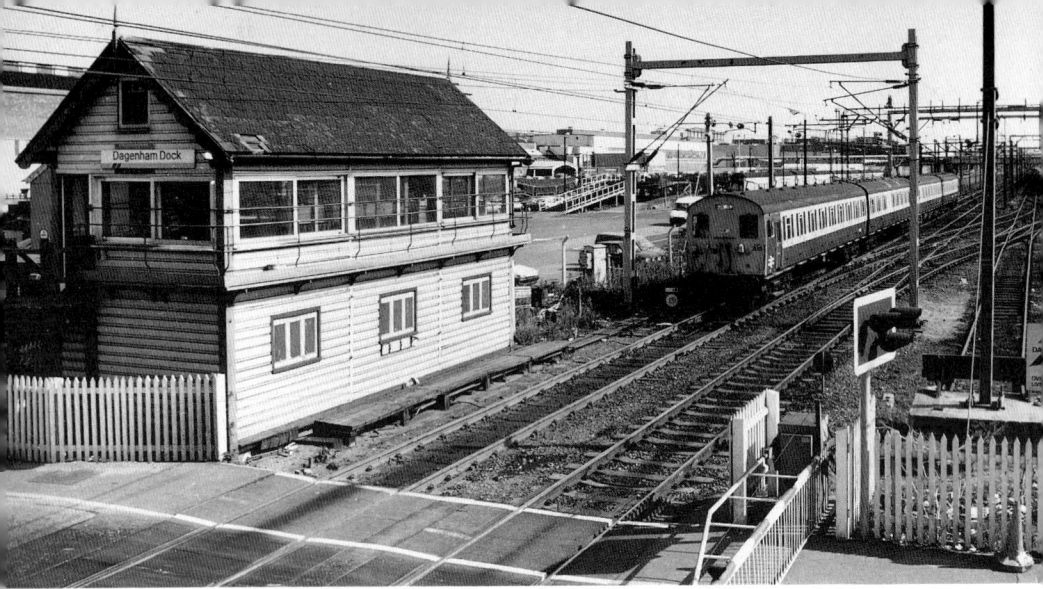

A 1901 vintage LT&SR signal box at Dagenham Dock.
Brian Morrison

Signalling

The range of signalling systems used today on Network SouthEast covers the whole spectrum of signalling technology from the oldest to the newest equipment. At one end of the spectrum is the venerable semaphore signalling in use on the line between Bletchley and Bedford while, at the other, experiments now being started to implement an Automatic Train Protection system.

The principal purpose of railway signalling is the need to keep trains from colliding with each other. Collisions must be prevented, either by preventing trains on the same track from colliding or by preventing trains on different tracks from making moves across each other's paths at the same time. In the former case it is done by maintaining a safe braking distance between trains; in the latter by ensuring that conflicting routes cannot be set up.

Trains were originally kept apart by what was known as the 'time interval' system. A train was only dispatched from a station after a fixed period of time had elapsed since the departure of the preceding train. Whilst this had the appearance of being able to keep trains from colliding with each other, there was no guarantee that the first train would not stop and allow the second train to catch it up. If the driver of the second train failed to see the first train in time, there was a very real risk of a serious collision.

More importantly for the railway companies the system also severely restricted the capacity of the line since, in the early days at least, the time interval between trains was fixed at ten minutes. Forced to reduce this, and to stem the growing public concern about accidents, the railways introduced what became the basis for all present day signalling systems - the concept of the block section.

The line was divided into sections or 'blocks' as they were, and still are, called. The entrance to each block was protected by a fixed signal displayed to the driver. The signal only showed a 'proceed' indication to a train if there was no other train in that section. Signals were controlled from cabins located at intervals along the line and the control of trains was passed from one cabin to the next as they passed along the line.

By the late nineteenth century block signalling was standard on most of the country's railways. Signals had also been standardised. A stop signal was a horizontal semaphore arm showing a co-acting red light at night. Proceed was indicated by tilting the arm at 45° either upwards or downwards and the display of a green light. An advance warning signal, known as a 'distant', was provided at many locations to give the driver warning of a red signal. These were also semaphore arms but had a fish tail end instead of a square end and showed a yellow light. Such semaphore signals can still be seen on parts of NSE (eg, Bletchley-Bedford).

Early signalling installations relied upon the skill and memory of the signalman to ensure the correct signals were displayed to drivers and on the drivers to obey them. If a signalman forgot where a train was, or could not see clearly that it had passed by his cabin, a mistake could be made. Drivers could and did pass signals at danger and there were some serious accidents until systems for locking signals and warning drivers of signal aspects were introduced.

The signalman was given instruments in his cabin which he used to remind him of whether he had a train under his control or not. These 'lock and block' instruments told him whether he had a train in his section. They were connected to the cabins on either side of him so that passing trains from one section to another was a co-operative act between signalmen of adjacent sections. Eventually, the presence of a train in a section could be detected by means of treadles operated by the wheels of the train as it passed a point in the section. The operation of a treadle would lock the signals protecting that section at danger until it was cleared.

The introduction of the electric telegraph allowed messages concerning the trains to be passed from one signal cabin to the next by the use of coded messages in the form of bell strokes. The type of train, its position in the section, even its destination could be transmitted in this way.

The most important development at this time was the requirement for co-operation between two signal boxes before a train could be signalled through a section. A train could not be admitted to the section ahead of a box until the signalman at the next box had 'accepted' it by the operation of the plunger in his cabin.

The next stage in the development of signalling was the introduction of track circuiting. This was a step further from the use of a treadle. The treadle acted only in a fixed position in the block section whereas the track circuit covered the whole section.

A weak electric current is passed through the rails of each block section and supplies a relay which is used to control the signal. The wheels and axles of a train arriving on the track shunt the circuit and de-energise the relay, which causes a danger signal to be shown. This has formed the basis for all present day signalling systems, allowing a visual indication of the presence of trains on the signalman's diagram as well as locking the signalling equipment against the inadvertent display of a 'proceed' indication over an occupied section.

Another important part of railway signalling systems is interlocking. This is the system by which it is impossible to offer a driver a proceed indication while a conflicting route is set up at a junction. An early form of this was first tried in 1860 at Kentish Town and later became standard railway equipment. The interlocking was achieved by mechanically linking the levels operating the points and signals so that a signal level could only be moved to show a proceed indication if the points on that route were correctly set and no other points or signals were offering a conflicting route.

On the modern systems being applied to NSE resignalling schemes today, the mechanical interlocking has been replaced by electronics - SSI or Solid State Interlocking. The mechanical links have been replaced by electronic systems which perform the same function without the need for large, cumbersome and difficult to maintain ironwork.

The standard signal familiar to observers all over Network SouthEast is the multi-aspect colour light signal. These range from the two aspect (red and green) signal seen on the more lightly used lines to the four aspect (red, yellow, green, yellow) type seen on the heavily trafficked lines.

The two-aspect signal is a straight replacement for the traditional semaphore signal and provides the driver with a simple stop or proceed indication. It is used over lines where all types of trains can operate but where the speeds of trains will be limited and their frequency comparatively low.

To allow more trains to run at faster speeds, it is necessary to provide drivers of the faster trains with an advance warning of the state of the road ahead. This is done by using three-aspect signals which show red, yellow and green aspects. The yellow aspect indicates that the section ahead is clear but that the one beyond may not be and the next signal is showing a red aspect. A green shows that at least two sections ahead are clear.

Line capacity can be further increased by providing shorter sections and more aspects. Many of the heavily used main lines out of London on the major NSE routes use four aspect signalling. A single yellow indicates one section ahead clear, two yellows indicate two sections clear and green, three or more sections ahead are clear. By this system trains of differing speeds can use the same track with the same high degree of safety regardless of their speeds. It also allows a line to be used to carry more trains at lower speeds than would be possible if the line had to be signalled for the speed of the fastest train ever to use it. This feature is useful for the dense suburban services which are an important part of Network SouthEast operations.

Many signals in use today are automatic in operation. They are controlled by the passage of trains. As a train clears a block section, the signal protecting that section registers that its track circuit has been vacated and automatically displays a proceed aspect. In multi-aspect signalled areas, the previous signals will also change their aspects automatically. Only at junctions is it necessary to introduce manual control systems.

The use of automatic signals allows much larger areas to be controlled from one signal box. Nowadays, in fact, the signal box is replaced by the control centre. Whole lines or wide areas can be controlled from one room and train movements can be signalled under the control of computers and solid state interlocking systems.

The development of control centres began in the 1920s with the introduction of power signalling at large locations on the Southern Railway. Instead of the traditional large levers operating the signals through rods and wires, smaller levers are used and points and signals operated by electric power. The levers were still mechanically interlocked to prevent conflicting moves being set up.

The next development was the introduction of relay interlocking during the 1930s. The mechanical interlocking was replaced by relays performing the same function. This allowed the levers to be dispensed with and push buttons or miniature switches to be used instead. The switches were placed on the signalman's diagram. This showed the position of trains and signals and displayed the signal indication and routes set up.

A further development was the introduction of the NX panel. Previous installations used thumb switches or buttons which acted to set up one route. The NX system (entrance/exit panel) was operated by the use of a push button at the entrance to a set of routes, the routes required being set up by the operation of a second button at the exit. A number of such installations are employed on Network SouthEast as on the line between London and Dover, for example.

The most modern signal control system on Network SouthEast is at Liverpool Street. It is known as the IECC (Integrated Electronic Control Centre). The centre was made operational in March 1989 and brought under its control the first part of the resignalling scheme for the Anglia region between Liverpool Street and Southend and Colchester.

When power signalling was introduced in the 1920s, larger areas could be controlled from one installation. The modern day power boxes and control centres are developments of this. West Hampstead Power Box is illustrated here. NSE

The IECC brings together the various uses for modern technology in the form of SSI and computer based control and monitoring systems. The SSI performs electronically the interlocking functions formerly carried out by relays while the control system uses computers to monitor and control train movements and to process and transmit information.

The biggest change in the IECC compared with earlier control rooms is that there is no longer a traditional signalman's diagram showing to any observer the picture of all the lines and signals controlled by the centre. Instead, VDUs (Visual Display Units) are provided in a series of individual workstations.

Each signalman is provided with a set of three screens which show the area under his command. Two of the screens cover the area in general while the third screen can be used to go into an area in close up and can show details of track circuit lengths and the identity and location of signals and equipment on the ground.

The signals are controlled through a tracker ball and seven push buttons. The principle is based on the NX system so that the tracker ball is used to locate the cursor on the screen at the entrance of a route. A 'set' button actuates the entrance and the cursor is moved to the exit of the route where the 'set' button is operated again. A second 'set' button and two 'cancel' buttons are provided, the duplication providing ease of use and flexibility. Three further buttons provide point control for normal, reverse and centre setting.

Along the bottom of the screen is a row of cursor operated 'buttons' which allow the screen information and close up facilities to be operated. There are also 'buttons' for removing from operation sections of track under engineering possessions.

A fourth screen is provided to allow the receipt of text messages and, with the use of a keyboard, to give the signalman the facility to interrogate the train describer system. New train descriptions can be inserted and the Automatic Route Setting system can be controlled manually.

Automatic Route Setting (ARS) was first tried out at Three Bridges control centre on the Southern Region. Simply put, the ARS signals the train according to the scheduled times in the timetable and the availability of the routes it requires. Under normal conditions it will receive the train's description and then send it through the correct route to its destination. If necessary it can be reprogrammed to carry out the routeing in a different way or at a different time, or it can be operated manually. The timetable element is linked to the BR national timetable database. There are also some stored emergency routines which will allow special movement options to be used when there is a disruption to the normal service.

The Integrated Electronic Control Centre at Liverpool Street, brought into use in March 1989. BR

Following the introduction of the first section of the new system at Liverpool Street, sections of the line will be converted in stages. A similar system will also be introduced over the Waterloo area resignalling scheme (WARS).

Work on the Waterloo scheme was marred by the collision at Clapham Junction. This has led to a reassessment of the work and a delay in the programme. Other recent accidents, like the one at Purley where a driver passed a signal at danger, have led to increased pressure for a more proactive safety system.

Means of preventing drivers from making errors in the reading of and reaction to signals have long occupied the minds of railway engineers. Eventually, an Automatic Warning System (AWS) was standardised throughout the system. It relies upon the use of a magnetic induction system which gives the driver an audible warning of the status of a signal aspect. A bell rings for a green signal and a horn sounds for a yellow or red signal. If the driver fails to cancel the warning horn within a set time, usually 15 seconds, the brakes will automatically apply.

The one disadvantage of this system is that it still relies upon the driver remembering to brake the train after he has cancelled a warning. The danger arises particularly in areas where the train is operating over densely trafficked lines and running under a succession of yellow signals. There have been a number of cases where drivers have passed signals at danger. To provide a more positive safety system, a trial of an Automatic Train Protection (ATP) system is being carried out on Network SouthEast.

ATP is already used in a number of ways on existing railways. The London Underground has a trainstop operating with each signal which will stop any train attempting to pass the signal at danger by operating a trip arm on the train. Electronic versions of this are used on the Victoria Line and other automatic metros around the world but it relies on the fact that all trains have a similar braking performance. This is not the case on a main line railway where freight trains of different weights and braking performances operate over the same lines as passenger trains, also with differing weights and braking performances.

ATP systems rely on a microprocessor on the train which keeps the details of the train's performance. On metros, this information is standard throughout the fleet. For railways with varying train types like Network SouthEast, information about the train weight and speed can be input by the driver at the start of the journey. The train speed will then be restricted to the maximum safe level permitted by its composition.

The transmission of information about the signals can be either continuous or intermittent. The continuous system is generally used on metros and other railways where trains have similar performance, like the French TGV railways. For Network SouthEast, the system to be tried is by means of beacons mounted on the track. As the train passes over each beacon, the state of the signals ahead is transmitted to the microprocessor. This gives the driver a target speed indication and monitors that the train is slowed down to this speed as necessary. If the train speed exceeds the permitted level, then the brakes will automatically apply.

One drawback of this scheme is that once the train has received the information from a beacon, it has no way of being told any changes until it reaches the beacon at the next signal. If a red signal changes to green, the train will still have the red information in the microprocessor and will still continue to brake. On a train without ATP, the driver would be able to resume normal speed as soon as he sees the red signal change to green.

A trial of this system is being installed on the Marylebone to Aylesbury section of Network SouthEast to see if it can be used without slowing up train speeds unnecessarily. It is also being installed on the main line out of Paddington to see its effect on high speed services. Useful information will be gained on how the equipment can be installed on an existing railway and how it performs in service. If the scheme is successful, it will be the start of a new era in railway signalling in Britain.

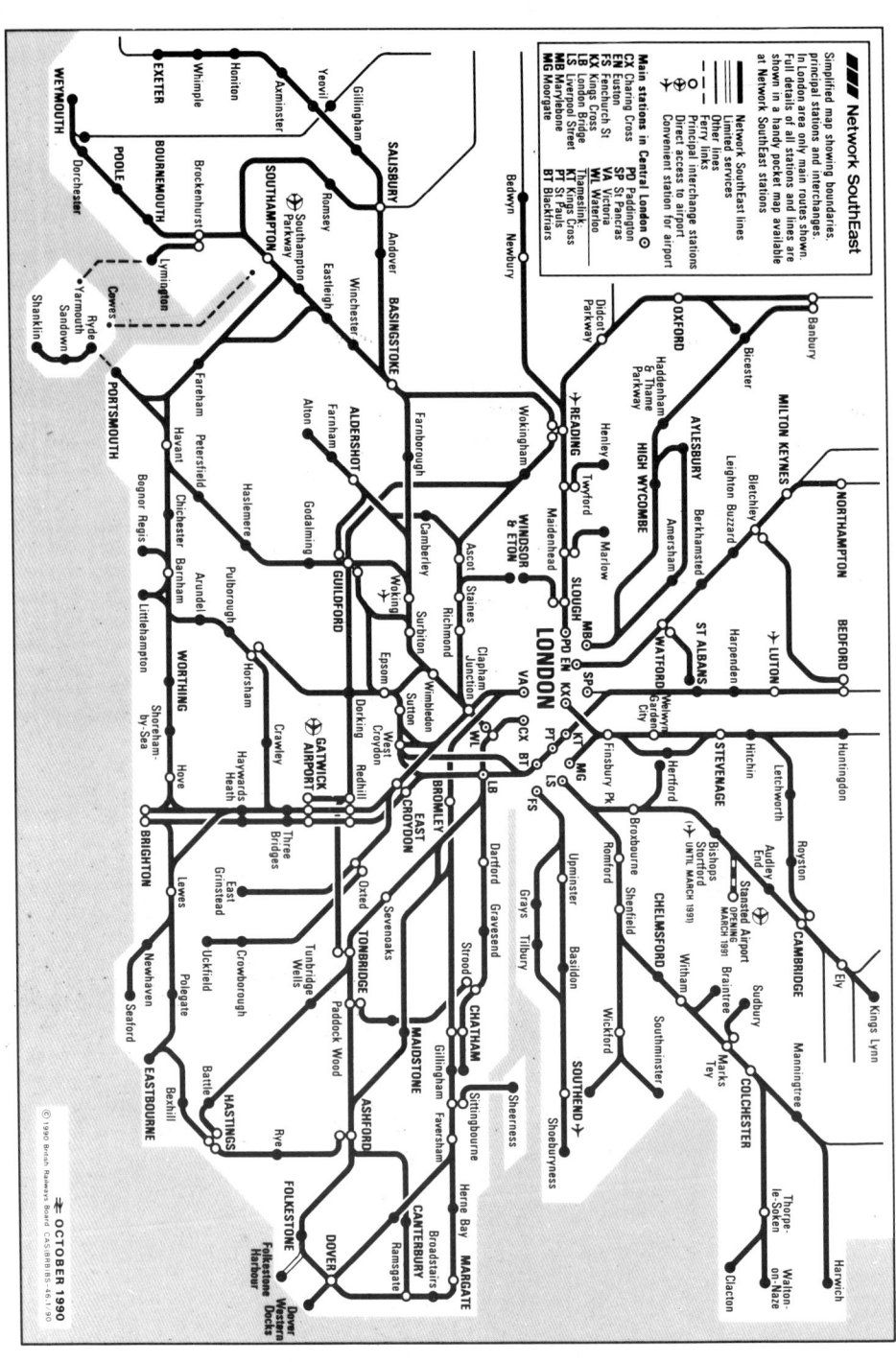